The Poetry of Ambrose Bierce - Volume 1

Ambrose Gwinnett Bierce had a diverse literary, military and journalistic career, during which his sardonic view of human nature ensured he was both frequently critical and frequently criticised. As a writer, his work included short stories, fables, editorials and his journalism, which was often controversial owing to his vehemence and acerbic style.

He was born on June 24th 1842 at Horse Cave Creek in Meigs Country, Ohio. His parents were poor and very religious but instilled in the young Bierce an abiding love of language and literature.

A year at the Kentucky Military Institute prepared him for the Civil War and a source of much of his acclaimed writing. Eventually he moved west to San Francisco where he married and began his literary career in earnest. A few years in England saw his work begin to publish in greater quantities

By 1891 although his marriage had fallen apart he had published 'An Occurrence at Owl Creek' his classic short story. To this he quickly added volumes of poetry and further volumes of stories and essays as well as a thriving career with the Hearst Organisation. In all his reputation was set as one of America's foremost literary creators.

At the age of 71, in 1913 Bierce departed from Washington, D.C., for a tour of the battlefields upon which he had fought during the civil war. He passed through Louisiana and Texas by December and was crossed into Mexico which was in the throes of revolution. He joined Pancho Villa's army as an observer. It was in Chihuahua where he wrote his last known communication dated 26th December 1913, closing with the words "as to me, I leave here tomorrow for an unknown destination" and then vanished without trace in what would become one of the most famous unexplained disappearances in American history.

Index of Contents
A Ballad Of Pikeville
A Bequest To Music
A Bit Of Science
A Black-List
A 'Born Leader Of Men'
A Bubble
A Builder
A Bulletin
A Caller
A Career In Letters
A Celebrated Case
A Challenge
A Cheating Preacher
A Commuted Sentence
A Controversialist
A Coward
A Critic
A Crocodile
A Culinary Candidate
A Dampened Ardor

A Demagogue
A Demand
A Dilemma
A Fair Division
A False Prophecy
A Fish Commissioner
A Fool
A Growler
A Guest
A Hasty Inference
A Hymn Of The Many
A Jack-At-All-Views
A Lacking Factor
A Lifted Finger
A Literary Hangman
'A Literary Method'
A Long-Felt Want
A Man
A 'Mass' Meeting
A Merciful Governor
A Military Incident
A Morning Fancy
A 'Mute Inglorious Milton'
A Nightmare
A Paradox
A Partisan's Protest
A Patter Song
A Pickbrain
A Poet's Father
A Poet's Hope
A Political Apostate
A Political Violet
A Possibility
A Prayer
A Promised Fast Train
A Question Of Eligibility
A Railroad Lackey
A Rear Elevation
A Rendezvous
A Reply To A Letter
A Retort
A 'Scion Of Nobility'
A Serenade
A Silurian Holiday
A Soaring Toad
A Social Call
A Society Leader
A Song In Praise
A Spade
A Study In Gray
A Vision Of Climate

A Vision Of Doom
A Vision Of Resurrection
A Volupatory
A Warning
A Welcome
A Wet Season
A Whipper-In
A Word To The Unwise
A Wreath Of Immortelles
A Year's Casualties
Accepted
Ad Cattonum
Ad Moodium
Adair Welcker, Poet
Again
Alone
An Actor
An Alibi
An Anarchist
An Apologue
An Art Critic
An Augury
An Average
An Enemy To Law And Order
An Epitaph
An Epitaph
An Example
An 'Exhibit'
An Exile
An Explanation
An Idler
An Imposter
An Inscription *(For a Proposed Monument in Washington)*
An Inscription *(For A Statue Of Napoleon, At West Point)*
An Interpretation
An Obituarian
An Offer Of Marriage
An Undress Uniform
An Unmerry Christmas
Another Plan
Another Way
Arbor Day
Arboriculture
Arma Virumque
Art
Arthur Mcewen
Aspiration
At Anchor
At The Close Of The Canvass
At The Eleventh Hour
At The 'National Encampment'

Authority
Azrael
Bats In Sunshine
Beecher
Bereavement
Bimetalism
'Black Bart'
Borrowed Brains
Business
By A Defeated Litigant
By False Pretenses
Cain
California
Carmelite
Censor Literarum
Charles And Peter
Christian
Codex Honoris
Consolation
Constancy
Contemplation
Contentment
Convalescent
Cooperation
Corrected News
Couplets
Creation
De Young - A Prophecy
Decalogue
Democracy
Dennis Kearney
Detected
Diagnosis
'Died Of A Rose'
Dies Irae
Disappointment
Discretion
Down Among The Dead Men
Egotist
Election Day
Elegy
Elixer Vitæ
Ambrose Bierce - A Short Biography

A Ballad Of Pikeville

Down in Southern Arizona where the Gila monster thrives,
And the 'Mescalero,' gifted with a hundred thousand lives,
Every hour renounces one of them by drinking liquid flame
The assassinating wassail that has given him his name;

Where the enterprising dealer in Caucasian hair is seen
To hold his harvest festival upon his village-green,
While the late lamented tenderfoot upon the plain is spread
With a sanguinary circle on the summit of his head;
Where the cactuses (or cacti) lift their lances in the sun,
And incautious jackass-rabbits come to sorrow as they run,
Lived a colony of settlers - old Missouri was the State
Where they formerly resided at a prehistoric date.
Now, the spot that had been chosen for this colonizing scheme
Was as waterless, believe me, as an Arizona stream.
The soil was naught but ashes, by the breezes driven free,
And an acre and a quarter were required to sprout a pea.
So agriculture languished, for the land would not produce,
And for lack of water, whisky was the beverage in use
Costly whisky, hauled in wagons many a weary, weary day,
Mostly needed by the drivers to sustain them on their way.
Wicked whisky! King of Evils! Why, O, why did God create
Such a curse and thrust it on us in our inoffensive state?
Once a parson came among them, and a holy man was he;
With his ailing stomach whisky wouldn't anywise agree;
So he knelt upon the mesa and he prayed with all his chin
That the Lord would send them water or incline their hearts to gin.
Scarcely was the prayer concluded ere an earthquake shook the land,
And with copious effusion springs burst out on every hand!
Merrily the waters gurgled, and the shock which gave them birth
Fitly was by some declared a temperance movement of the earth.
Astounded by the miracle, the people met that night
To celebrate it properly by some religious rite;
And 'tis truthfully recorded that before the moon had sunk
Every man and every woman was devotionally drunk.
A half a standard gallon (says history) per head
Of the best Kentucky prime was at that ceremony shed.
O, the glory of that country! O, the happy, happy folk.
By the might of prayer delivered from Nature's broken yoke!
Lo! the plains to the horizon all are yellowing with rye,
And the corn upon the hill-top lifts its banners to the sky!
Gone the wagons, gone the drivers, and the road is grown to grass,
Over which the incalescent Bourbon did aforetime pass.
Pikeville (that's the name they've given, in their wild, romantic way,
To that irrigation district) now distills, statistics say,
Something like a hundred gallons, out of each recurrent crop,
To the head of population - and consumes it, every drop!

A Bequest To Music

'Let music flourish!' So he said and died.
Hark! ere he's gone the minstrelsy begins:
The symphonies ascend, a swelling tide,
Melodious thunders fill the welkin wide
The grand old lawyers, chinning on their chins!

A Bit Of Science

What! photograph in colors? 'Tis a dream
And he who dreams it is not overwise,
If colors are vibration they but seem,
And have no being. But if Tyndall lies,
Why, come, then - photograph my lady's eyes.
Nay, friend, you can't; the splendor of their blue,
As on my own beclouded orbs they rest,
To naught but vibratory motion's due,
As heart, head, limbs and all I am attest.
How could her eyes, at rest themselves, be making
In me so uncontrollable a shaking?

A Black-List

'Resolved that we will post,' the tradesmen say,
'All names of debtors who do never pay.'
'Whose shall be first?' inquires the ready scribe
'Who are the chiefs of the marauding tribe?'
Lo! high Parnassus, lifting from the plain,
Upon his hoary peak, a noble fane!
Within that temple all the names are scrolled
Of village bards upon a slab of gold;
To that bad eminence, my friend, aspire,
And copy thou the Roll of Fame, entire.
Yet not to total shame those names devote,
But add in mercy this explaining note:
'These cheat because the law makes theft a crime,
And they obey all laws but laws of rhyme.'

A 'Born Leader Of Men'

Tuckerton Tamerlane Morey Mahosh
Is a statesman of world-wide fame,
With a notable knack at rhetorical bosh
To glorify somebody's name
Somebody chosen by Tuckerton's masters
To succor the country from divers disasters
Portentous to Mr. Mahosh.
Percy O'Halloran Tarpy Cabee
Is in the political swim.
He cares not a button for men, not he:
Great principles captivate him
Principles cleverly cut out and fitted
To Percy's capacity, duly submitted,
And fought for by Mr. Cabee.

Drusus Turn Swinnerton Porfer Fitzurse
Holds office the most of his life.
For men nor for principles cares he a curse,
But much for his neighbor's wife.
The Ship of State leaks, but he doesn't pump any,
Messrs. Mahosh, Cabee & Company
Pump for good Mr. Fitzurse.

A Bubble

Mrs. Mehitable Marcia Moore
Was a dame of superior mind,
With a gown which, modestly fitting before,
Was greatly puffed up behind.
The bustle she wore was ingeniously planned
With an inspiration bright:
It magnified seven diameters and
Was remarkably nice and light.
It was made of rubber and edged with lace
And riveted all with brass,
And the whole immense interior space
Inflated with hydrogen gas.
The ladies all said when she hove in view
Like the round and rising moon:
'She's a stuck up thing!' which was partly true,
And men called her the Captive Balloon.
To Manhattan Beach for a bath one day
She went and she said: 'O dear!
If I leave off this what will people say?
I shall look so uncommonly queer!'
So a costume she had accordingly made
To take it all nicely in,
And when she appeared in that suit arrayed,
She was greeted with many a grin.
Proudly and happily looking around,
She waded out into the wet,
But the water was very, very profound,
And her feet and her forehead met!
As her bubble drifted away from the shore,
On the glassy billows borne,
All cried: 'Why, where is Mehitable Moore?
I saw her go in, I'll be sworn!'
Then the bulb it swelled as the sun grew hot,
Till it burst with a sullen roar,
And the sea like oil closed over the spot
Farewell, O Mehitable Moore!

A Builder

I saw the devil - he was working free:
A customs-house he builded by the sea.
'Why do you this?' The devil raised his head;
'Churches and courts I've built enough,' he said.

A Bulletin

'Lothario is very low,'
So all the doctors tell.
Nay, nay, not so - he will be, though,
If ever he get well.

A Caller

'Why, Goldenson, you're looking very well.'
Said Death as, strolling through the County Jail,
He entered that serene assassin's cell
And hung his hat and coat upon a nail.
'I think that life in this secluded spot
Agrees with men of your trade, does it not?'
'Well, yes,' said Goldenson, 'I can't complain:
Life anywhere - provided it is mine
Agrees with me; but I observe with pain
That still the people murmur and repine.
It hurts their sense of harmony, no doubt,
To see a persecuted man grow stout.'
'O no, 'tis not your growing stout,' said Death,
'Which makes these malcontents complain and scold
They like you to be, somehow, scant of breath.
What they object to is your growing old.
And - though indifferent to lean or fat
I don't myself entirely favor that.'
With brows that met above the orbs beneath,
And nose that like a soaring hawk appeared,
And lifted lip, uncovering his teeth,
The Mamikellikiller coldly sneered:
'O, so you don't! Well, how will you assuage
Your spongy passion for the blood of age?'
Death with a clattering convulsion, drew
His coat on, hatted his unmeated pow,
Unbarred the door and, stepping partly through,
Turned and made answer: 'I will show you how.
I'm going to the Bench you call Supreme
And tap the old women who sit there and dream.'

A Career In Letters

When Liberverm resigned the chair

Of This or That in college, where
For two decades he'd gorged his brain
With more than it could well contain,
In order to relieve the stress
He took to writing for the press.
Then Pondronummus said, 'I'll help
This mine of talent to devel'p;'
And straightway bought with coin and credit
The Thundergust for him to edit.
The great man seized the pen and ink
And wrote so hard he couldn't think;
Ideas grew beneath his fist
And flew like falcons from his wrist.
His pen shot sparks all kinds of ways
Till all the rivers were ablaze,
And where the coruscations fell
Men uttered words I dare not spell.
Eftsoons with corrugated brow,
Wet towels bound about his pow,
Locked legs and failing appetite,
He thought so hard he couldn't write.
His soaring fancies, chickenwise,
Came home to roost and wouldn't rise.
With dimmer light and milder heat
His goose-quill staggered o'er the sheet,
Then dragged, then stopped; the finish came
He couldn't even write his name.
The Thundergust in three short weeks
Had risen, roared, and split its cheeks.
Said Pondronummus, 'How unjust!
The storm I raised has laid my dust!'
When, Moneybagger, you have aught
Invested in a vein of thought,
Be sure you've purchased not, instead,
That salted claim, a bookworm's head.

A Celebrated Case

Way down in the Boom Belt lived Mrs. Roselle;
A person named Petrie, he lived there as well;
But Mr. Roselle he resided away
Sing tooral iooral iooral iay.
Once Mrs. Roselle in her room was alone:
The flesh of her flesh and the bone of her bone
Neglected the wife of his bosom to woo
Sing tooral iooral iooral ioo.
Then Petrie, her lover, appeared at the door,
Remarking: 'My dear; I don't love you no more.'
'That's awfully rough,' said the lady, 'on me
Sing tooral iooral iooral iee.'

'Come in, Mr. Petrie,' she added, 'pray do:
Although you don't love me no more, I love you.
Sit down while I spray you with vitriol now
Sing tooral iooral iooral iow.'
Said Petrie: 'That liquid I know won't agree
With my beauty, and then you'll no longer love me;
So spray and be 'O, what a word he did say!
Sing tooral iooral iooral iay.
She deluged his head and continued to pour
Till his bonny blue eyes, like his love, were no more.
It was seldom he got such a hearty shampoo
Sing tooral iooral iooral ioo.
Then Petrie he rose and said: 'Mrs. Roselle,
I have an engagement and bid you farewell.'
'You see,' she began to explain - but not he!
Sing tooral, iooral, iooral iee.
The Sheriff he came and he offered his arm,
Saying, 'Sorry I am for disturbin' you, marm,
But business is business.' Said she, 'So they say
Sing tooral, iooral, iooral iay.'
The Judge on the bench he looked awfully stern;
The District Attorney began to attorn;
The witnesses lied and the lawyers - O my!
Sing tooral, iooral, iooral iyi.
The chap that defended her said: 'It's our claim
That he loved us no longer and told us the same.
What else than we did could we decently do?
Sing tooral, iooral, iooral ioo.'
The District Attorney, sarcastic, replied:
'We loved you no longer - that can't be denied.

Not having no eyes we may dote on you now
Sing tooral, iooral, iooral iow.'
The prisoner wept to entoken her fears;
The sockets of Petrie were flooded with tears.
O heaven-born Sympathy, bully for you!
Sing tooral, iooral, iooral ioo.
Four jurors considered the prisoner mad,
And four thought her victim uncommonly bad,
And four that the acid was all in his eye
Sing rum tiddy iddity iddity hi.

A Challenge
A bull imprisoned in a stall
Broke boldly the confining wall,
And found himself, when out of bounds,
Within a washerwoman's grounds.
Where, hanging on a line to dry,
A crimson skirt inflamed his eye.

With bellowings that woke the dead,
He bent his formidable head,
With pointed horns and gnarly forehead;
Then, planting firm his shoulders horrid,
Began, with rage made half insane,
To paw the arid earth amain,
Flinging the dust upon his flanks
In desolating clouds and banks,
The while his eyes' uneasy white
Betrayed his doubt what foe the bright
Red tent concealed, perchance, from sight.
The garment, which, all undismayed,
Had never paled a single shade,
Now found a tongue - a dangling sock,
Left carelessly inside the smock:
'I must insist, my gracious liege,
That you'll be pleased to raise the siege:
My colors I will never strike.
I know your sex - you're all alike.
Some small experience I've had
You're not the first I've driven mad.'

A Cheating Preacher

Munhall, to save my soul you bravely try,
Although, to save my soul, I can't say why.
'Tis naught to you, to me however much
Why, bless it! you might save a million such
Yet lose your own; for still the 'means of grace'
That you employ to turn us from the place
By the arch-enemy of souls frequented
Are those which to ensnare us he invented!
I do not say you utter falsehoods - I
Would scorn to give to ministers the lie:
They cannot fight - their calling has estopped it.
True, I did not persuade them to adopt it.
But, Munhall, when you say the Devil dwells
In all the breasts of all the infidels
Making a lot of individual Hells
In gentlemen instinctively who shrink
From thinking anything that you could think,
You talk as I should if some world I trod
Where lying is acceptable to God.
I don't at all object - forbid it Heaven!
That your discourse you temperately leaven
With airy reference to wicked souls
Cursing impenitent on glowing coals,
Nor quarrel with your fancy, blithe and fine,
Which represents the wickedest as mine.
Each ornament of style my spirit eases:

The subject saddens, but the manner pleases.
But when you 'deal damnation round' 'twere sweet
To think hereafter that you did not cheat.
Deal, and let all accept what you allot 'em.
But, blast you! you are dealing from the bottom!

A Commuted Sentence

Boruck and Waterman upon their grills
In Hades lay, with many a sigh and groan,
Hotly disputing, for each swore his own
Were clearly keener than the other's ills.
And, truly, each had much to boast of - bone
And sinew, muscle, tallow, nerve and skin,
Blood in the vein and marrow in the shin,
Teeth, eyes and other organs (for the soul
Has all of these and even a wagging chin)
Blazing and coruscating like a coal!
For Lower Sacramento, you remember,
Has trying weather, even in mid-December.
Now this occurred in the far future. All
Mankind had been a million ages dead,
And each to her reward above had sped,
Each to his punishment below, I call
That quite a just arrangement. As I said,
Boruck and Waterman in warmest pain
Crackled and sizzed with all their might and main.
For, when on earth, they'd freed a scurvy host
Of crooks from the State prison, who again
Had robbed and ravaged the Pacific Coast
And (such the felon's predatory nature)
Even got themselves into the Legislature.
So Waterman and Boruck lay and roared
In Hades. It is true all other males
Felt the like flames and uttered equal wails,
But did not suffer them; whereas they bored
Each one the other. But indeed my tale's
Not getting on at all. They lay and browned
Till Boruck (who long since his teeth had ground
Away and spoke Gum Arabic and made
Stump speeches even in praying) looked around
And said to Bob's incinerated shade:
'Your Excellency, this is mighty hard on
The inventors of the unpardonable pardon.'
The other soul - his right hand all aflame,
For 'twas with that he'd chiefly sinned, although
His tongue, too, like a wick was working woe
To the reserve of tallow in his frame
Said, with a sputtering, uncertain flow,
And with a gesture like a shaken torch:

'Yes, but I'm sure we'll not much longer scorch.
Although this climate is not good for Hope,
Whose joyous wing 'twould singe, I think the porch
Of Hell we'll quit with a pacific slope.
Last century I signified repentance
And asked for commutation of our sentence.'

Even as he spoke, the form of Satan loomed
In sight, all crimson with reflections's fire,
Like some tall tower or cathedral spire
Touched by the dawn while all the earth is gloomed
In mists and shadows of the night time. 'Sire,'
Said Waterman, his agitable wick
Still sputtering, 'what calls you back so quick?
It scarcely was a century ago
You left us.' 'I have come to bring,' said Nick,
'St. Peter's answer (he is never slow
In correspondence) to your application
For pardon - pardon me! for commutation.
'He says that he's instructed to reply
(And he has so instructed me) that sin
Like yours - and this poor gentleman's who's in
For bad advice to you - comes rather high;
But since, apparently, you both begin
To feel some pious promptings to the right,
And fain would turn your faces to the light,
Eternity seems all too long a term.
So 'tis commuted to one-half. I'm quite
Prepared, when that expires, to free the worm
And quench the fire.' And, civilly retreating,
He left them holding their protracted meeting.

A Controversialist
I've sometimes wished that Ingersoll were wise
To hold his tongue, nor rail against the skies;
For when he's made a point some pious dunce
Like Bartlett of the Bulletin 'replies.'
I brandish no iconoclastic fist,
Nor enter the debate an atheist;
But when they say there is a God I ask
Why Bartlett, then, is suffered to exist.
Even infidels that logic might resent,
Saying: 'There's no place for his punishment
That's worse than earth.' But humbly I submit
That he would make a hell wherever sent.

A Coward

By hardihood to rise and fear to strike,
And fitly to rebuke his sins decrees,
That, hide from others with what care he please,
Night sha'n't be black enough nor earth so wide
That from himself himself can ever hide!
Hard fate indeed to feel at every breath
His burden of identity till death!
No moment's respite from the immortal load,
To think himself a serpent or a toad,
Or dream, with a divine, ecstatic glow,
He's long been dead and canonized a crow!

A Critic

That from you, neighbor! to whose vacant lot
Each rhyming literary knacker scourges
His cart-compelling Pegasus to trot,
As folly, fame or famine smartly urges?
Admonished by the stimulating goad,
How gaily, lo! the spavined crow-bait prances
Its cart before it - eager to unload
The dead-dog sentiments and swill-tub fancies.
Gravely the sweating scavenger pulls out
The tail-board of his curst imagination,
Shoots all his rascal rubbish, and, no doubt,
Thanks Fortune for so good a dumping-station.
To improve your property, the vile cascade
Your thrift invites to make a higher level.
In vain: with tons of garbage overlaid,
Your baseless bog sinks slowly to the devil.
'Rubbish may be shot here' familiar sign!
I seem to see it in your every column.
You have your wishes, but if I had mine
'Twould to your editor mean something solemn.

A Crocodile

Nay, Peter Robertson, 'tis not for you
To blubber o'er Max Taubles for he's dead.
By Heaven! my hearty, if you only knew
How better is a grave-worm in the head
Than brains like yours - how far more decent, too,
A tomb in far Corea than a bed
Where Peter lies with Peter, you would covet
His happier state and, dying, learn to love it.
In the recesses of the silent tomb
No Maunderings of yours disturb the peace.
Your mental bag-pipe, droning like the gloom
Of Hades audible, perforce must cease

From troubling further; and that crack o' doom,
Your mouth, shaped like a long bow, shall release
In vain such shafts of wit as it can utter
The ear of death can't even hear them flutter.

A Culinary Candidate
A cook adorned with paper cap,
Or waiter with a tray,
May be a worthy kind of chap
In his way,
But when we want one for Recorder,
Then, Mr. Walton, take our order.

A Dampened Ardor
The Chinatown at Bakersfield
Was blazing bright and high;
The flames to water would not yield,
Though torrents drenched the sky
And drowned the ground for miles around
The houses were so dry.
Then rose an aged preacher man
Whom all did much admire,
Who said: 'To force on you my plan
I truly don't aspire,
But streams, it seems, might quench these beams
If turned upon the fire.'
The fireman said: 'This hoary wight
His folly dares to thrust
On us! 'Twere well he felt our might
Nay, he shall feel our must!'
With jet of wet and small regret
They laid that old man's dust.

A Demagogue
Yawp, yawp, yawp!
Under the moon and sun.
It's aye the rabble,
And I to gabble,
And hey! for the tale that is never done.
'Chant, chant, chant!
To woo the reluctant vote.
I would I were dead
And my say were said
And my song were sung to its ultimate note.
'Stab, stab, stab!

Ah! the weapon between my teeth
I'm sick of the flash of it;
See how the slash of it
Misses the foeman to mangle the sheath!
'Boom, boom, boom!
I'm beating the mammoth drum.
My nethermost tripes
I blow into the pipes
It's oh! for the honors that never come!'
'Twas the dolorous blab
Of a tramping 'scab'
'Twas the eloquent Swift
Of the marvelous gift
The wild, weird, wonderful gift of gab!

A Demand

You promised to paint me a picture,
Dear Mat,
And I was to pay you in rhyme.
Although I am loth to inflict your
Most easy of consciences, I'm
Of opinion that fibbing is awful,
And breaking a contract unlawful,
Indictable, too, as a crime,
A slight and all that.
If, Lady Unbountiful, any
Of that
By mortals called pity has part
In your obdurate soul - if a penny
You care for the health of my heart,
By performing your undertaking
You'll succor that organ from breaking
And spare it for some new smart,
As puss does a rat.
Do you think it is very becoming,
Dear Mat,
To deny me my rights evermore
And bless you! if I begin summing
Your sins they will make a long score!
You never were generous, madam,
If you had been Eve and I Adam
You'd have given me naught but the core,
And little of that.
Had I been content with a Titian,
A cat
By Landseer, a meadow by Claude,
No doubt I'd have had your permission
To take it by purchase abroad.
But why should I sail o'er the ocean

For Landseers and Claudes? I've a notion
All's bad that the critics belaud.
I wanted a Mat.
Presumption's a sin, and I suffer
For that:
But still you did say that sometime,
If I'd pay you enough (here's enougher
That's more than enough) of rhym
You'd paint me a picture. I pay you
Hereby in advance; and I pray you
Condone, while you can, your crime,
And send me a Mat.
But if you don't do it I warn you,
Dear Mat,
I'll raise such a clamor and cry
On Parnassus the Muses will scorn you
As mocker of poets and fly
With bitter complaints to Apollo:
'Her spirit is proud, her heart hollow,
Her beauty' - they'll hardly deny,
On second thought, that!

A Dilemma

Filled with a zeal to serve my fellow men,
For years I criticised their prose and verges:
Pointed out all their blunders of the pen,
Their shallowness of thought and feeling; then
Damned them up hill and down with hearty curses!
They said: 'That's all that he can do - just sneer,
And pull to pieces and be analytic.
Why doesn't he himself, eschewing fear,
Publish a book or two, and so appear
As one who has the right to be a critic?
'Let him who knows it all forbear to tell
How little others know, but show his learning.'
The public added: 'Who has written well
May censure freely' quoting Pope. I fell
Into the trap and books began out-turning,
Books by the score - fine prose and poems fair,
And not a book of them but was a terror,
They were so great and perfect; though I swear
I tried right hard to work in, here and there,
(My nature still forbade) a fault or error.
'Tis true, some wretches, whom I'd scratched, no doubt,
Professed to find - but that's a trifling matter.
Now, when the flood of noble books was out
I raised o'er all that land a joyous shout,
Till I was thought as mad as any hatter!
(Why hatters all are mad, I cannot say.

'T were wrong in their affliction to revile 'em,
But truly, you'll confess 'tis very sad
We wear the ugly things they make. Begad,
They'd be less mischievous in an asylum!)
'Consistency, thou art a' - well, you're paste!
When next I felt my demon in possession,
And made the field of authorship a waste,
All said of me: 'What execrable taste,
To rail at others of his own profession!'
Good Lord! where do the critic's rights begin
Who has of literature some clear-cut notion,
And hears a voice from Heaven say: 'Pitch in'?
He finds himself - alas, poor son of sin
Between the devil and the deep blue ocean!

A Fair Division
Another Irish landlord gone to grass,
Slain by the bullets of the tenant class!
Pray, good agrarians, what wrong requires
Such foul redress? Between you and the squires
All Ireland's parted with an even hand
For you have all the ire, they all the land.

A False Prophecy
Dom Pedro, Emperor of far Brazil
(Whence coffee comes and the three-cornered nut),
They say that you're imperially ill,
And threatened with paralysis. Tut-tut!
Though Emperors are mortal, nothing but
A nimble thunderbolt could catch and kill
A man predestined to depart this life
By the assassin's bullet, bomb or knife.
Sir, once there was a President who freed
Ten million slaves; and once there was a Czar
Who freed five times as many serfs. Sins breed
The means of punishment, and tyrants are
Hurled headlong out of the triumphal car
If faster than the law allows they speed.
Lincoln and Alexander struck a rut;
You freed slaves too. Paralysis - tut-tut!

A Fish Commissioner
Great Joseph D. Redding - illustrious name!
Considered a fish-horn the trumpet of Fame.
That goddess was angry, and what do you think?

Her trumpet she filled with a gallon of ink,
And all through the Press, with a devilish glee,
She sputtered and spattered the name of J.D.

A Fool

Says Anderson, Theosophist:
'Among the many that exist
In modern halls,
Some lived in ancient Egypt's clime
And in their childhood saw the prime
Of Karnak's walls.'
Ah, Anderson, if that is true
'T is my conviction, sir, that you
Are one of those
That once resided by the Nile,
Peer to the sacred Crocodile,
Heir to his woes.
My judgment is, the holy Cat
Mews through your larynx (and your hat)
These many years.
Through you the godlike Onion brings
Its melancholy sense of things,
And moves to tears.
In you the Bull divine again
Bellows and paws the dusty plain,
To nature true.
I challenge not his ancient hate
But, lowering my knurly pate,
Lock horns with you.
And though Reincarnation prove
A creed too stubborn to remove,
And all your school
Of Theosophs I cannot scare
All the more earnestly I swear
That you're a fool.
You'll say that this is mere abuse
Without, in fraying you, a use.
That's plain to see
With only half an eye. Come, now,
Be fair, be fair, consider how
It eases me!

A Growler

Judge Shafter, you're an aged man, I know,
And learned too, I doubt not, in the law;
And a head white with many a winter's snow
(I wish, however that your heart would thaw)

Claims reverence and honor; but the jaw
That's always wagging with a word malign,
Nagging and scolding every one in sight
As harshly as a jaybird in a pine,
And with as little sense of wrong and right
As animates that irritable creature,
Is not a very venerable feature.
You damn all witnesses, all jurors too
(And swear at the attorneys, I suppose,
But that's commendable) 'till all is blue';
And what it's all about, the good Lord knows,
Not you; but all the hotter, fiercer glows
Your wrath for that - as dogs the louder howl
With only moonshine to incite their rage,
And bears with more ferocious menace growl,
Even when their food is flung into the cage.
Reform, your Honor, and forbear to curse us.
Lest all men, hearing you, cry: 'Ecce ursus!'

A Guest

Death, are you well? I trust you have no cough
That's painful or in any way annoying
No kidney trouble that may carry you off,
Or heart disease to keep you from enjoying
Your meals and ours. 'T were very sad indeed
To have to quit the busy life you lead.
You've been quite active lately for so old
A person, and not very strong - appearing.
I'm apprehensive, somehow, that my bold,
Bad brother gave you trouble in the spearing.
And my two friends - I fear, sir, that you ran
Quite hard for them, especially the man.
I crave your pardon: 'twas no fault of mine;
If you are overworked I'm sorry, very.
Come in, old man, and have a glass of wine.
What shall it be - Marsala, Port or Sherry?
What! just a mug of blood? That's funny grog
To ask a friend for, eh? Well, take it, hog!

A Hasty Inference

The Devil one day, coming up from the Pit,
All grimy with perspiration,
Applied to St. Peter and begged he'd admit
Him a moment for consultation.
The Saint showed him in where the Master reclined
On the throne where petitioners sought him;
Both bowed, and the Evil One opened his mind

Concerning the business that brought him:
'For ten million years I've been kept in a stew
Because you have thought me immoral;
And though I have had my opinion of you,
You've had the best end of the quarrel.
'But now - well, I venture to hope that the past
With its misunderstandings we'll smother;
And you, sir, and I, sir, be throned here at last
As equals, the one to the other.'
'Indeed!' said the Master (I cannot convey
A sense of his tone by mere letters)
'What makes you presume you'll be bidden to stay
Up here on such terms with your betters?'
'Why, sure you can't mean it!' said Satan. 'I've seen
How Stanford and Crocker you've nourished,
And Huntington - bless me! the three like a green
Umbrageous great bay-tree have flourished.
They are fat, they are rolling in gold, they command
All sources and well-springs of power;
You've given them houses, you've given them land
Before them the righteous all cower.'
'What of that?' 'What of that?' cried the Father of Sin;
'Why, I thought when I saw you were winking
At crimes such as theirs that perhaps you had been
Converted to my way of thinking.'

A Hymn Of The Many

God's people sorely were oppressed,
I heard their lamentations long;
I hear their singing, clear and strong,
I see their banners in the West!
The captains shout the battle-cry,
The legions muster in their might;
They turn their faces to the light,
They lift their arms, they testify:
'We sank beneath the Master's thong,
Our chafing chains were ne'er undone;
Now clash your lances in the sun
And bless your banners with a song!
'God bides his time with patient eyes
While tyrants build upon the land;
He lifts his face, he lifts his hand,
And from the stones his temples rise.
'Now Freedom waves her joyous wing
Beyond the foemen's shields of gold.
March forward, singing, for, behold,
The right shall rule while God is king!'

A Jack-At-All-Views

So, Estee, you are still alive! I thought
That you had died and were a blessed ghost
I know at least your coffin once was bought
With Railroad money; and 'twas said by most
Historians that Stanford made a boast
The seller 'threw you in.' That goes for naught
Man takes delight in fancy's fine inventions,
And woman too, 'tis said, if they are French ones.
Do you remember, Estee-ah, 'twas long
And long ago! how fierce you grew and hot
When anything impeded the straight, strong,
Wild sweep of the great billow you had got
Atop of, like a swimmer bold? Great Scott!
How fine your wavemanship! How loud your song
Of 'Down with railroads!' When the wave subsided
And left you stranded you were much divided.
Then for a time you were content to wade
The waters of the 'robber barons'' moat.
To fetch, and carry was your humble trade,
And ferry Stanford over in a boat,
Well paid if he bestowed the kindly groat
And spoke you fair and called you pretty maid.
And when his stomach seemed a bit unsteady
You got your serviceable basin ready.
Strange man! how odd to see you, smug and spruce,
There at Chicago, burrowed in a Chair,
Not made to measure and a deal too loose,
And see you lift your little arm and swear
Democracy shall be no more! If it's a fair
And civil question, and not too abstruse,
Were you elected as a 'robber baron,'
Or as a Communist whose teeth had hair on?

A Lacking Factor

'You acted unwisely,' I cried, 'as you see
By the outcome.' He calmly eyed me:
'When choosing the course of my action,' said he,
'I had not the outcome to guide me.'

A Lifted Finger

What! you whip rascals? you, whose gutter blood
Bears, in its dark, dishonorable flood,
Enough of prison - birds' prolific germs
To serve a whole eternity of terms?
You, for whose back the rods and cudgels strove

Ere yet the ax had hewn them from the grove?
You, the De Young whose splendor bright and brave
Is phosphorescence from another's grave
Till now unknown, by any chance or luck,
Even to the hearts at which you, feebly struck?
You whip a rascal out of office? you
Whose leadless weapon once ignobly blew
Its smoke in six directions to assert
Your lack of appetite for others' dirt?
Practice makes perfect: when for fame you thirst,
Then whip a rascal. Whip a cripple first.
Or, if for action you're less free than bold
Your palms both brimming with dishonest gold
Entrust the castigation that you've planned,
As once before, to woman's idle hand.
So in your spirit shall two pleasures join
To slake the sacred thirst for blood and coin.
Blood? Souls have blood, even as the body hath,
And, spilled, 'twill fertilize the field of wrath.
Lo! in a purple gorge of yonder hills,
Where o'er a grave a bird its day-song stills,
A woman's blood, through roses ever red,
Mutely appeals for vengeance on your head.
Slandered to death to serve a sordid end,
She called you murderer and called me friend.
Now, mark you, libeler, this course if you
Dare to maintain, or rather to renew;
If one short year's immunity has made
You blink again the perils of your trade
The ghastly sequence of the maddened 'knave,'
The hot encounter and the colder grave;
If the grim, dismal lesson you ignore
While yet the stains are fresh upon your floor,
And calmly march upon the fatal brink
With eyes averted to your trail of ink,
Counting unkind the services of those
Who pull, to hold you back, your stupid nose,
The day for you to die is not so far,
Or, at the least, to live the thing you are!
Pregnant with possibilities of crime,
And full of felons for all coming time,
Your blood's too precious to be lightly spilt
In testimony to a venial guilt.
Live to get whelpage and preserve a name

No praise can sweeten and no lie unshame.
Live to fulfill the vision that I see
Down the dim vistas of the time to be:
A dream of clattering beaks and burning eyes
Of hungry ravens glooming all the skies;
A dream of gleaming teeth and foetid breath

Of jackals wrangling at the feast of death;
A dream of broken necks and swollen tongues
The whole world's gibbets loaded with De Youngs!

A Literary Hangman
Beneath his coat of dirt great Neilson loves
To hide the avenging rope.
He handles all he touches without gloves,
Excepting soap.

'A Literary Method'
His poems Riley says that he indites
Upon an empty stomach. Heavenly Powers,
Feed him throat-full: for what the beggar writes
Upon his empty stomach empties ours!

A Long-Felt Want
Dimly apparent, through the gloom
Of Market-street's opaque simoom,
A queue of people, parti-sexed,
Awaiting the command of 'Next!'
A sidewalk booth, a dingy sign:
'Teeth dusted nice - five cents a shine.'

A Man
Pennoyer, Governor of Oregon,
Casting to South his eye across the bourne
Of his dominion (where the Palmiped,
With leathers 'twixt his toes, paddles his marsh,
Amphibious) saw a rising cloud of hats,
And heard a faint, far sound of distant cheers
Below the swell of the horizon. 'Lo,'
Cried one, 'the President! the President!'
All footed webwise then took up the word
The hill tribes and the tribes lacustrine and
The folk riparian and littoral,
Cried with one voice: 'The President! He comes!'
And some there were who flung their headgear up
In emulation of the Southern mob;
While some, more soberly disposed, stood still
And silently had fits; and others made
Such reverent genuflexions as they could,
Having that climate in their bones. Then spake

The Court Dunce, humbly, as became him: 'Sire,
If thou, as heretofore thou hast, wilt deign
To reap advantage of a fool's advice
By action ordered after nature's way,
As in thy people manifest (for still
Stupidity's the only wisdom) thou
Wilt get thee straight unto to the border land
To mark the President's approach with such
Due, decent courtesy as it shall seem
We have in custom the best warrant for.'
Pennoyer, Governor of Oregon,
Eyeing the storm of hats which darkened all
The Southern sky, and hearing far hurrahs
Of an exulting people, answered not.
Then some there were who fell upon their knees,
And some upon their Governor, and sought
Each in his way, by blandishment or force,
To gain his action to their end. 'Behold,'
They said, 'thy brother Governor to South
Met him even at the gateway of his realm,
Crook-kneed, magnetic-handed and agrin,
Backed like a rainbow - all things done in form
Of due observance and respect. Shall we
Alone of all his servitors refuse
Swift welcome to our master and our lord?'
Pennoyer, Governor of Oregon,
Answered them not, but turned his back to them
And as if speaking to himself, the while
He started to retire, said: 'He be damned!'
To that High Place o'er Portland's central block,
Where the Recording Angel stands to view

The sinning world, nor thinks to move his feet
Aside and look below, came flocking up
Inferior angels, all aghast, and cried:
'Pennoyer, Governor of Oregon,
Has said, O what an awful word! too bad
To be by us repeated!' 'Yes, I know,'
Said the superior bird - 'I heard it too,
And have already booked it. Pray observe.'
Splitting the giant tome, whose covers fell
Apart, o'ershadowing to right and left
The Eastern and the Western world, he showed
The newly written entry, black and big,
Upon the credit side of thine account,
Pennoyer, Governor of Oregon.

A 'Mass' Meeting
It was a solemn rite as e'er

Was seen by mortal man.
The celebrants, the people there,
Were all Republican.
There Estee bent his grizzled head,
And General Dimond, too,
And one - 'twas Reddick, some one said,
Though no one clearly knew.
I saw the priest, white-robed and tall
(Assistant, Father Stow)
He was the pious man men call
Dan Burns of Mexico.
Ah, 'twas a high and holy rite
As any one could swear.
'What does it mean?' I asked a wight
Who knelt apart in prayer.
'A mass for the repose,' he said,
'Of Colonel Markham's' - 'What,
Is gallant Colonel Markham dead?
'Tis sad, 'tis sad, God wot!'
'A mass' repeated he, and rose
To go and kneel among
The worshipers 'for the repose
Of Colonel Markham's tongue.'

A Merciful Governor
Standing within the triple wall of Hell,
And flattening his nose against a grate
Behind whose brazen bars he'd had to dwell
A thousand million ages to that date,
Stoneman bewailed his melancholy fate,
And his big tear-drops, boiling as they fell,
Had worn between his feet, the record mentions,
A deep depression in the 'good intentions.'
Imperfectly by memory taught how
For prayer in Hell is a lost art - he prayed,
Uplifting his incinerated brow
And flaming hands in supplication's aid.
'O grant,' he cried, 'my torment may be stayed
In mercy, some short breathing spell allow!
If one good deed I did before my ghosting,
Spare me and give Delmas a double roasting.'
Breathing a holy harmony in Hell,
Down through the appalling clamors of the place,
Charming them all to willing concord, fell
A Voice ineffable and full of grace:
'Because of all the law-defying race
One single malefactor of the cell
Thou didst not free from his incarceration,
Take thou ten thousand years of condonation.'

Back from their fastenings began to shoot
The rusted bolts; with dreadful roar, the gate
Laboriously turned; and, black with soot,
The extinguished spirit passed that awful strait,
And as he legged it into space, elate,
Muttered: 'Yes, I remember that galoot
I'd signed his pardon, ready to allot it,
But stuck it in my desk and quite forgot it.'

A Military Incident

Dawn heralded the coming sun
Fort Douglas was computing
The minutes - and the sunrise gun
Was manned for his saluting.
The gunner at that firearm stood,
The which he slowly loaded,
When, bang! I know not how it could,
But sure the charge exploded!
Yes, to that veteran's surprise
The gun went off sublimely,
And both his busy arms likewise
Went off with it, untimely.
Then said that gunner to his mate
(He was from Ballyshannon):
'Bedad, the sun's a minute late,
Accardin' to this cannon!'

A Morning Fancy

I drifted (or I seemed to) in a boat
Upon the surface of a shoreless sea
Whereon no ship nor anything did float,
Save only the frail bark supporting me;
And that - it was so shadowy - seemed to be
Almost from out the very vapors wrought
Of the great ocean underneath its keel;
And all that blue profound appeared as naught
But thicker sky, translucent to reveal,
Miles down, whatever through its spaces glided,
Or at the bottom traveled or abided.
Great cities there I saw - of rich and poor,
The palace and the hovel; mountains, vales,
Forest and field, the desert and the moor,
Tombs of the good and wise who'd lived in jails,
And seas of denser fluid, white with sails
Pushed at by currents moving here and there
And sensible to sight above the flat
Of that opaquer deep. Ah, strange and fair

The nether world that I was gazing at
With beating heart from that exalted level,
And - lest I founder - trembling like the devil!
The cities all were populous: men swarmed
In public places - chattered, laughed and wept;
And savages their shining bodies warmed
At fires in primal woods. The wild beast leapt
Upon its prey and slew it as it slept.
Armies went forth to battle on the plain
So far, far down in that unfathomed deep
The living seemed as silent as the slain,
Nor even the widows could be heard to weep.
One might have thought their shaking was but laughter;
And, truly, most were married shortly after.
Above the wreckage of that silent fray
Strange fishes swam in circles, round and round
Black, double-finned; and once a little way
A bubble rose and burst without a sound
And a man tumbled out upon the ground.
Lord! 'twas an eerie thing to drift apace
On that pellucid sea, beneath black skies
And o'er the heads of an undrowning race;
And when I woke I said - to her surprise
Who came with chocolate, for me to drink it:
'The atmosphere is deeper than you think it.'

A 'Mute Inglorious Milton'
'O, I'm the Unaverage Man,
But you never have heard of me,
For my brother, the Average Man, outran
My fame with rapiditee,
And I'm sunk in Oblivion's sea,
But my bully big brother the world can span
With his wide notorietee.
I do everything that I can
To make 'em attend to me,
But the papers ignore the Unaverage Man
With a weird uniformitee.'
So sang with a dolorous note
A voice that I heard from the beach;
On the sable waters it seemed to float
Like a mortal part of speech.
The sea was Oblivion's sea,
And I cried as I plunged to swim:
'The Unaverage Man shall reside with me.'
But he didn't - I stayed with him!

A Nightmare

I dreamed that I was dead. The years went by:
The world forgot that such a man as I
Had ever lived and written: other names
Were hailed with homage, in their turn to die.
Out of my grave a giant beech upgrew.
Its roots transpierced my body, through and through,
My substance fed its growth. From many lands
Men came in troops that giant tree to view.
'T was sacred to my memory and fame
My monument. But Allen Forman came,
Filled with the fervor of a new untruth,
And carved upon the trunk his odious name!

A Paradox

'If life were not worth having,' said the preacher,
''T would have in suicide one pleasant feature.'
'An error,' said the pessimist, 'you're making:
What's not worth having cannot be worth taking.

A Partisan's Protest

O statesmen, what would you be at,
With torches, flags and bands?
You make me first throw up my hat,
And then my hands.

A Patter Song

There was a cranky Governor
His name it wasn't Waterman.
For office he was hotter than
The love of any lover, nor
Was Boruck's threat of aiding him
Effective in dissuading him
This pig-headed, big-headed, singularly self-conceited Governor Nonwaterman.
To citrus fairs, et caetera,
He went about philandering,
To pride of parish pandering.
He knew not any better - ah,
His early education had
Not taught the abnegation fad
The wool-witted, bull-witted, fabulously feeble-minded king of gabble-gandering!
He conjured up, ad libitum,
With postures energetical,
One day (this is prophetical)
His graces, to exhibit 'em.

He straddled in each attitude,
Four parallels of latitude
The slab-footed, crab-footed, galloping gregarian, of presence unaesthetical!
An ancient cow, perceiving that
His powers of agility
Transcended her ability
(A circumstance for grieving at)
Upon her horns engrafted him
And to the welkin wafted him
The high-rolling, sky-rolling, hurtling hallelujah-lad of peerless volatility!

A Pickbrain

What! imitate me, friend? Suppose that you
With agony and difficulty do
What I do easily - what then? You've got
A style I heartily wish I had not.
If I from lack of sense and you from choice
Grieve the judicious and the unwise rejoice,
No equal censure our deserts will suit
We both are fools, but you're an ape to boot!

A Poet's Father

Welcker, I'm told, can boast a father great
And honored in the service of the State.
Public Instruction all his mind employs
He guides its methods and its wage enjoys.
Prime Pedagogue, imperious and grand,
He waves his ferule o'er a studious land
Where humming youth, intent upon the page,
Thirsting for knowledge with a noble rage,
Drink dry the whole Pierian spring and ask
To slake their fervor at his private flask.
Arrested by the terror of his frown,
The vaulting spit-ball drops untimely down;
The fly impaled on the tormenting pin
Stills in his awful glance its dizzy din;
Beneath that stern regard the chewing-gum
Which writhed and squeaked between the teeth is dumb;
Obedient to his will the dunce-cap flies
To perch upon the brows of the unwise;
The supple switch forsakes the parent wood
To settle where 'twill do the greatest good,
Puissant still, as when of old it strove
With Solomon for spitting on the stove
Learned Professor, variously great,
Guide, guardian, instructor of the State
Quick to discern and zealous to correct

The faults which mar the public intellect
From where of Siskiyou the northern bound
Is frozen eternal to the sunless ground
To where in San Diego's torrid clime
The swarthy Greaser swelters in his grime
Beneath your stupid nose can you not see
The dunce whom once you dandled on your knee?
O mighty master of a thousand schools,
Stop teaching wisdom, or stop breeding fools.

A Poet's Hope
'Twas a weary looking mortal, and he wandered near the portal
Of the melancholy City of the Discontented Dead.
He was pale and worn exceeding and his manner was unheeding,
As if it could not matter what he did nor what he said.
'Sacred stranger' I addressed him with a reverence befitting
The austere, unintermitting, dread solemnity he wore;
'Tis the custom, too, prevailing in that vicinage when hailing
One who possibly may be a person lately 'gone before'
'Sacred stranger, much I ponder on your evident dejection,
But my carefulest reflection leaves the riddle still unread.
How do you yourself explain your dismal tendency to wander
By the melancholy City of the Discontented Dead?'
Then that solemn person, pausing in the march that he was making,
Roused himself as if awaking, fixed his dull and stony eye
On my countenance and, slowly, like a priest devout and holy,
Chanted in a mournful monotone the following reply:
'O my brother, do not fear it; I'm no disembodied spirit
I am Lampton, the Slang Poet, with a price upon my head.
I am watching by this portal for some late lamented mortal
To arise in his disquietude and leave his earthy bed.
'Then I hope to take possession and pull in the earth above me
And, renouncing my profession, ne'er be heard of any more.
For there's not a soul to love me and no living thing respects me,
Which so painfully affects me that I fain would 'go before.''
Then I felt a deep compassion for the gentleman's dejection,
For privation of affection would refrigerate a frog.
So I said: 'If nothing human, and if neither man nor woman
Can appreciate the fashion of your merit - buy a dog.'

A Political Apostate
Good friend, it is with deep regret I note
The latest, strangest turning of your coat;
Though any way you wear that mental clout
The seamy side seems always to be out.
Who could have thought that you would e'er sustain
The Southern shotgun's arbitrary reign!

Your sturdy hand assisting to replace
The broken yoke on a delivered race;
The ballot's purity no more your care,
With equal privilege to dark and fair.
To Yesterday a traitor, to To-day
You're constant but the better to betray
To-morrow. Your convictions all are naught
But the wild asses of the world of thought,
Which, flying mindless o'er the barren plain,
Perceive at last they've nothing so to gain,
And, turning penitent upon their track,
Economize their strength by flying back.
Ex-champion of Freedom, battle-lunged,
No more, red-handed, or at least red-tongued,
Brandish the javelin which by others thrown
Clove Sambo's heart to quiver in your own!
Confess no more that when his blood was shed,
And you so sympathetically bled,
The bow that spanned the mutual cascade
Was but the promise of a roaring trade
In offices. Your fingering now the trigger
Shows that you knew your Negro was a nigger!
Ad hominem this argumentum runs:
Peace! let us fire another kind of guns.
I grant you, friend, that it is very true
The Blacks are ignorant and sable, too.
What then? One way of two a fool must vote,
And either way with gentlemen of note
Whose villain feuds the fact attest too well
That pedagogues nor vice nor error quell.
The fiercest controversies ever rage
When Miltons and Salmasii engage.
No project wide attention ever drew
But it disparted all the learned crew.
As through their group the cleaving line's prolonged
With fiery combatants each field is thronged.
In battle-royal they engage at once
For guidance of the hesitating dunce.
The Titans on the heights contend full soon
On this side Webster and on that Calhoun,
The monstrous conflagration of their fight
Startling the day and splendoring the night!
Both are unconquerable - one is right.
Will't keep the pigmy, if we make him strong,
From siding with a giant in the wrong?
When Genius strikes for error, who's afraid
To arm poor Folly with a wooden blade?
O Rabelais, you knew it all! your good
And honest judge (by men misunderstood)
Knew to be right there was but one device
Less fallible than ignorance - the dice.

The time must come - Heaven expedite the day!
When all mankind shall their decrees obey,
And nations prosper in their peaceful sway.

A Political Violet
Come, Stanford, let us sit at ease
And talk as old friends do.
You talk of anything you please,
And I will talk of you.
You recently have said, I hear,
That you would like to go
To serve as Senator. That's queer!
Have you told William Stow?
Once when the Legislature said:
'Go, Stanford, and be great!'
You lifted up your Jovian head
And everlooked the State.
As one made leisurely awake,
You lightly rubbed your eyes
And answered: 'Thank you - please to make
A note of my surprise.
'But who are they who skulk aside,
As to get out of reach,
And in their clothing strive to hide
Three thousand dollars each?
'Not members of your body, sure?
No, that can hardly be:
All statesmen, I suppose, are pure.
What! there are rogues? Dear me!'
You added, you'll recall, that though
You were surprised and pained,
You thought, upon the whole, you'd go,
And in that mind remained.
Now, what so great a change has wrought
That you so frankly speak
Of 'seeking' honors once unsought
Because you 'scorned to seek'?
Do you not fear the grave reproof
In good Creed Haymond's eye?
Will Stephen Gage not stand aloof
And pass you coldly by?
O, fear you not that Vrooman's lich
Will rise from earth and point
At you a scornful finger which
May lack, perchance, a joint?
Go, Stanford, where the violets grow,
And join their modest train.

Await the work of William Stow

And be surprised again.

A Possibility
If the wicked gods were willing
(Pray it never may be true!)
That a universal chilling
Should ensue
Of the sentiment of loving,
If they made a great undoing
Of the plan of turtle-doving,
Then farewell all poet-lore,
Evermore.
If there were no more of billing
There would be no more of cooing
And we all should be but owls
Lonely fowls
Blinking wonderfully wise,
With our great round eyes
Sitting singly in the gloaming and no longer two and two,
As unwilling to be wedded as unpracticed how to woo;
With regard to being mated,
Asking still with aggravated
Ungrammatical acerbity: 'To who? To who?'

A Prayer
Sweet Spirit of Cesspool, hear a mother's prayer:
Her terrors pacify and offspring spare!
Upon Silurians alone let fall
(And God in Heaven have mercy on them all!)
The red revenges of your fragrant breath,
Hot with the flames invisible of death.
Sing in each nose a melody of smells,
And lead them snoutwise to their several hells!

A Promised Fast Train
I turned my eyes upon the Future's scroll
And saw its pictured prophecies unroll.
I saw that magical life-laden train
Flash its long glories o'er Nebraska's plain.
I saw it smoothly up the mountain glide.
'O happy, happy passengers!' I cried.
For Pleasure, singing, drowned the engine's roar,
And Hope on joyous pinions flew before.
Then dived the train adown the sunset slope
Pleasure was silent and unseen was Hope.

Crashes and shrieks attested the decay
That greed had wrought upon that iron way.
The rusted rails broke down the rotting ties,
And clouds of flying spikes obscured the skies.
My coward eyes I drew away, distressed,
And fixed them on the terminus to - West,
Where soon, its melancholy tale to tell,
One bloody car-wheel wabbled in and fell!

A Question Of Eligibility
It was a bruised and battered chap
The victim of some dire mishap,
Who sat upon a rock and spent
His breath in this ungay lament:
'Some wars - I've frequent heard of such
Has beat the everlastin' Dutch!
But never fight was fit by man
To equal this which has began
In our (I'm in it, if you please)
Academy of Sciences.
For there is various gents belong
To it which go persistent wrong,
And loving the debates' delight
Calls one another names at sight.
Their disposition, too, accords
With fighting like they all was lords!
Sech impulses should be withstood:
'Tis scientific to be good.
''Twas one of them, one night last week,
Rose up his figure for to speak:
'Please, Mr. Chair, I'm holding here
A resolution which, I fear,
Some ancient fossils that has bust
Their cases and shook off their dust
To sit as Members here will find
Unpleasant, not to say unkind.'
And then he read it every word,
And silence fell on all which heard.
That resolution, wild and strange,
Proposed a fundamental change,
Which was that idiots no more
Could join us as they had before!
'No sooner was he seated than
The members rose up, to a man.
Each chap was primed with a reply
And tried to snatch the Chairman's eye.
They stomped and shook their fists in air,
And, O, what words was uttered there!
'The Chair was silent, but at last

He hove up his proportions vast
And stilled them tumults with a look
By which the undauntedest was shook.
He smiled sarcastical and said:
'If Argus was the Chair, instead
Of me, he'd lack enough of eyes
Each orator to recognize!
And since, denied a hearing, you
Might maybe undertake to do
Each other harm before you cease,
I've took some steps to keep the peace:
I've ordered out - alas, alas,
That Science e'er to such a pass
Should come! I've ordered out the gas!'
'O if a tongue or pen of fire
Was mine I could not tell entire
What the ensuin' actions was.
When swollered up in darkness' jaws
We fit and fit and fit and fit,
And everything we felt we hit!
We gouged, we scratched and we pulled hair,
And O, what words was uttered there!
And when at last the day dawn came
Three hundred Scientists was lame;
Two hundred others couldn't stand,
They'd been so careless handled, and
One thousand at the very least
Was spread upon the floor deceased!
'Twere easy to exaggerate,
But lies is things I mortal hate.
'Such, friends, is the disaster sad
Which has befel the Cal. Acad.
And now the question is of more
Importance than it was before:
Shall vacancies among us be
To idiots threw open free?'

A Railroad Lackey

Ben Truman, you're a genius and can write,
Though one would not suspect it from your looks.
You lack that certain spareness which is quite
Distinctive of the persons who make books.
You show the workmanship of Stanford's cooks
About the region of the appetite,
Where geniuses are singularly slight.
Your friends the Chinamen are understood,
Indeed, to speak of you as 'belly good.'
Still, you can write - spell, too, I understand
Though how two such accomplishments can go,

Like sentimental schoolgirls, hand in hand
Is more than ever I can hope to know.
To have one talent good enough to show
Has always been sufficient to command
The veneration of the brilliant band
Of railroad scholars, who themselves, indeed,
Although they cannot write, can mostly read.
There's Towne and Fillmore, Goodman and
Steve Gage, Ned Curtis of Napoleonic face,
Who used to dash his name on glory's page
'A.M.' appended to denote his place
Among the learned. Now the last faint trace
Of Nap. is all obliterate with age,
And Ned's degree less precious than his wage.
He says: 'I done it,' with his every breath.
'Thou canst not say I did it,' says Macbeth.
Good land! how I run on! I quite forgot
Whom this was meant to be about; for when
I think upon that odd, unearthly lot
Not quite Creedhaymonds, yet not wholly men
I'm dominated by my rebel pen
That, like the stubborn bird from which 'twas got,
Goes waddling forward if I will or not.
To leave your comrades, Ben, I'm now content:
I'll meet them later if I don't repent.
You've writ a letter, I observe - nay, more,
You've published it - to say how good you think
The coolies, and invite them to come o'er
In thicker quantity. Perhaps you drink
No corporation's wine, but love its ink;
Or when you signed away your soul and swore
On railrogue battle-fields to shed your gore
You mentally reserved the right to shed
The raiment of your character instead.
You're naked, anyhow: unragged you stand
In frank and stark simplicity of shame.

And here upon your flank, in letters grand,
The iron has marked you with your owner's name.
Needless, for none would steal and none reclaim.
But 'Leland $tanford' is a pretty brand,
Wrought by an artist with a cunning hand
But come - this naked unreserve is flat:
Don your habiliment - you're fat, you're fat!

A Rear Elevation
Once Moses (in Scripture the story is told)
Entreated the favor God's face to behold.
Compassion divine the petition denied

Lest vision be blasted and body be fried.
Yet this much, the Record informs us, took place:
Jehovah, concealing His terrible face,
Protruded His rear from behind a great rock,
And edification ensued without shock.
So godlike Salvini, lest worshipers die,
Averting the blaze of his withering eye,
Tempers his terrors and shows to the pack
Of feeble adorers the broad of his back.
The fires of their altars, which, paled and declined
Before him, burn all the more brightly behind.
O happy adorers, to care not at all
Where fawning may tickle or lip-service fall!

A Rendezvous

Nightly I put up this humble petition:
'Forgive me, O Father of Glories,
My sins of commission, my sins of omission,
My sins of the Mission Dolores.'

A Reply To A Letter

O nonsense, parson - tell me not they thrive
And jubilate who follow your dictation.
The good are the unhappiest lot alive
I know they are from careful observation.
If freedom from the terrors of damnation
Lengthens the visage like a telescope,
And lacrymation is a sign of hope,
Then I'll continue, in my dreadful plight,
To tread the dusky paths of sin, and grope
Contentedly without your lantern's light;
And though in many a bog beslubbered quite,
Refuse to flay me with ecclesiastic soap.
You say 'tis a sad world, seeing I'm condemned,
With many a million others of my kidney.
Each continent's Hammed, Japheted and Shemmed
With sinners - worldlings like Sir Philip Sidney
And scoffers like Voltaire, who thought it bliss
To simulate respect for Genesis
Who bent the mental knee as if in prayer,
But mocked at Moses underneath his hair,
And like an angry gander bowed his head to hiss.
Seeing such as these, who die without contrition,
Must go to-beg your pardon, sir - perdition,
The sons of light, you tell me, can't be gay,
But count it sin of the sort called omission
The groan to smother or the tear to stay

Or fail to - what is that they live by? pray.
So down they flop, and the whole serious race is
Put by divine compassion on a praying basis.
Well, if you take it so to heart, while yet
Our own hearts are so light with nature's leaven,
You'll weep indeed when we in Hades sweat,
And you look down upon us out of Heaven.
In fancy, lo! I see your wailing shades
Thronging the crystal battlements. Cascades
Of tears spring singing from each golden spout,
Run roaring from the verge with hoarser sound,
Dash downward through the glimmering profound,
Quench the tormenting flame and put the Devil out!
Presumptuous ass! to you no power belongs
To pitchfork me to Heaven upon the prongs
Of a bad pen, whose disobedient sputter,
With less of ink than incoherence fraught
Befits the folly that it tries to utter.
Brains, I observe, as well as tongues, can stutter:
You suffer from impediment of thought.
When next you 'point the way to Heaven,' take care:
Your fingers all being thumbs, point, Heaven knows where!
Farewell, poor dunce! your letter though I blame,
Bears witness how my anger I can tame:
I've called you everything except your hateful name!

A Retort

As vicious women think all men are knaves,
And shrew-bound gentlemen discourse of slaves;
As reeling drunkards judge the world unsteady
And idlers swear employers ne'er get ready
Thieves that the constable stole all they had,
The mad that all except themselves are mad;
So, in another's clear escutcheon shown,
Barnes rails at stains reflected from his own;
Prates of 'docility,' nor feels the dark
Ring round his neck - the Ralston collar mark.
Back, man, to studies interrupted once,
Ere yet the rogue had merged into the dunce.
Back, back to Yale! and, grown with years discreet,
The course a virgin's lust cut short, complete.
Go drink again at the Pierian pool,
And learn - at least to better play the fool.
No longer scorn the draught, although the font,
Unlike Pactolus, waters not Belmont.

A 'Scion Of Nobility'

Come, sisters, weep! our Baron dear,
Alas! has run away.
If always we had kept him here
He had not gone astray.
Painter and grainer it were vain
To say he was, before;
And if he were, yet ne'er again
He'll darken here a door.
We mourn each matrimonial plan
Even tradesmen join the cry:
He was so promising a man
Whenever he did buy.
He was a fascinating lad,
Deny it all who may;
Even moneyed men confess he had
A very taking way.
So from our tables he is gone
Our tears descend in showers;
We loved the very fat upon.
His kidneys, for 'twas ours.
To women he was all respect
To duns as cold as ice;
No lady could his suit reject,
No tailor get its price.
He raised our hope above the sky;
Alas! alack! and O!
That one who worked it up so high
Should play it down so low!

A Serenade

'Sas agapo sas agapo,'
He sang beneath her lattice.
''Sas agapo'?' she murmured - 'O,
I wonder, now, what that is!'
Was she less fair that she did bear
So light a load of knowledge?
Are loving looks got out of books,
Or kisses taught in college?
Of woman's lore give me no more
Than how to love, in many
A tongue men brawl: she speaks them all
Who says 'I love,' in any.

A Silurian Holiday

'Tis Master Fitch, the editor;
He takes an holiday.
Now wherefore, venerable sir,

So resolutely gay?
He lifts his head, he laughs aloud,
Odzounds! 'tis drear to see!
'Because the Boodle-Scribbler crowd
Will soon be far from me.
'Full many a year I've striven well
To freeze the caitiffs out
By making this good town a Hell,
But still they hang about.
'They maken mouths and eke they grin
At the dollar limit game;
And they are holpen in that sin
By many a wicked dame.
'In sylvan bowers hence I'll dwell
My bruised mind to ease.
Farewell, ye urban scenes, farewell!
Hail, unfamiliar trees!'
Forth Master Fitch did bravely hie,
And all the country folk
Besought him that he come not nigh
The deadly poison oak!
He smiled a cheerful smile (the day
Was straightway overcast)
The poison oak along his way
Was blighted as he passed!

A Soaring Toad

So, Governor, you would not serve again
Although we'd all agree to pay you double.
You find it all is vanity and pain
One clump of clover in a field of stubble
One grain of pleasure in a peck of trouble.
'Tis sad, at your age, having to complain
Of disillusion; but the fault is whose
When pigmies stumble, wearing giants' shoes?
I humbly told you many moons ago
For high preferment you were all unfit.
A clumsy bear makes but a sorry show
Climbing a pole. Let him, judicious, sit
With dignity at bottom of his pit,
And none his awkwardness will ever know.
Some beasts look better, and feel better, too,
Seen from above; and so, I think, would you.
Why, you were mad! Did you suppose because
Our foolish system suffers foolish men
To climb to power, make, enforce the laws,
And, it is whispered, break them now and then,
We love the fellows and respect them when
We've stilled the volume of our loud hurrahs?

When folly blooms we trample it the more
For having fertilized it heretofore.
Behold yon laborer! His garb is mean,
His face is grimy, but who thinks to ask
The measure of his brains? 'Tis only seen
He's fitted for his honorable task,
And so delights the mind. But let him bask
In droll prosperity, absurdly clean
Is that the man whom we admired before?
Good Lord, how ignorant, and what a bore!
Better for you that thoughtless men had said
(Noting your fitness in the humbler sphere):
'Why don't they make him Governor?' instead
Of, 'Why the devil did they?' But I fear
My words on your inhospitable ear
Are wasted like a sermon to the dead.
Still, they may profit you if studied well:
You can't be taught to think, but may to spell.

A Social Call

Well, well, old Father Christmas, is it you,
With your thick neck and thin pretense of virtue?
Less redness in the nose - nay, even some blue
Would not, I think, particularly hurt you.
When seen close to, not mounted in your car,
You look the drunkard and the pig you are.
No matter, sit you down, for I am not
In a gray study, as you sometimes find me.
Merry? O, no, nor wish to be, God wot,
But there's another year of pain behind me.
That's something to be thankful for: the more
There are behind, the fewer are before.
I know you, Father Christmas, for a scamp,
But Heaven endowed me at my soul's creation
With an affinity to every tramp
That walks the world and steals its admiration.
For admiration is like linen left
Upon the line - got easiest by theft.
Good God! old man, just think of it! I've stood,
With brains and honesty, some five-and-twenty
Long years as champion of all that's good,
And taken on the mazzard thwacks a-plenty.
Yet now whose praises do the people bawl?
Those of the fellows whom I live to maul!
Why, this is odd! the more I try to talk
Of you the more my tongue grows egotistic
To prattle of myself! I'll try to balk
Its waywardness and be more altruistic.
So let us speak of others - how they sin,

And what a devil of a state they 're in!
That's all I have to say. Good-bye, old man.
Next year you possibly may find me scolding
Or miss me altogether: Nature's plan
Includes, as I suppose, a final folding
Of these poor empty hands. Then dropp a tear
To think they'll never box another ear.

A Society Leader

'The Social World'! O what a world it is
Where full-grown men cut capers in the German,
Cotillion, waltz, or what you will, and whizz
And spin and hop and sprawl about like mermen!
I wonder if our future Grant or Sherman,
As these youths pass their time, is passing his
If eagles ever come from painted eggs,
Or deeds of arms succeed to deeds of legs.
I know they tell us about Waterloo:
How, 'foremost fighting,' fell the evening's dancers.
I don't believe it: I regard it true
That soldiers who are skillful in 'the Lancers'
Less often die of cannon than of cancers.
Moreover, I am half-persuaded, too,
That David when he danced before the Ark
Had the reporter's word to keep it dark.
Ed. Greenway, you fatigue. Your hateful name
Like maiden's curls, is in the papers daily.
You think it, doubtless, honorable fame,
And contemplate the cheap distinction gaily,
As does the monkey the blue-painted tail he
Believes becoming to him. 'Tis the same
With men as other monkeys: all their souls
Crave eminence on any kind of poles.
But cynics (barking tribe!) are all agreed
That monkeys upon poles performing capers
Are not exalted, they are only 'treed.'
A glory that is kindled by the papers
Is transient as the phosphorescent vapors
That shine in graveyards and are seen, indeed,
But while the bodies that supply the gas
Are turning into weeds to feed an ass.
One can but wonder sometimes how it feels
To be an ass - a beast we beat condignly
Because, like yours, his life is in his heels
And he is prone to use them unbenignly.
The ladies (bless them!) say you dance divinely.
I like St. Vitus better, though, who deals
His feet about him with a grace more just,
And hops, not for he will, but for he must.

Doubtless it gratifies you to observe
Elbowy girls and adipose mamas
All looking adoration as you swerve
This way and that; but prosperous papas
Laugh in their sleeves at you, and their ha-has,
If heard, would somewhat agitate your nerve.
And dames and maids who keep you on their shelves
Don't seem to want a closer tie themselves.
Gods! what a life you live! by day a slave
To your exacting back and urgent belly;
Intent to earn and vigilant to save
By night, attired so sightly and so smelly,
With countenance as luminous as jelly,
Bobbing and bowing! King of hearts and knave
Of diamonds, I'd bet a silver brick
If brains were trumps you'd never take a trick.

A Song In Praise

Hail, blessed Blunder! golden idol, hail!
Clay-footed deity of all who fail.
Celestial image, let thy glory shine,
Thy feet concealing, but a lamp to mine.
Let me, at seasons opportune and fit,
By turns adore thee and by turns commit.
In thy high service let me ever be
(Yet never serve thee as my critics me)
Happy and fallible, content to feel
I blunder chiefly when to thee I kneel.
But best felicity is his thy praise
Who utters unaware in works and ways
Who laborare est orare proves,
And feels thy suasion wheresoe'er he moves,
Serving thy purpose, not thine altar, still,
And working, for he thinks it his, thy will.
If such a life with blessings be not fraught,
I envy Peter Robertson for naught.

A Spade

Precursor of our woes, historic spade,
What dismal records burn upon thy blade!
On thee I see the maculating stains
Of passengers' commingled blood and brains.
In this red rust a widow's curse appears,
And here an orphan tarnished thee with tears.
Upon thy handle sanguinary bands
Reveal the clutching of thine owner's hands
When first he wielded thee with vigor brave

To cut a sod and dig a people's grave
(For they who are debauched are dead and ought,
In God's name, to be hid from sight and thought.)
Within thee, as within a magic glass,
I seem to see a foul procession pass
Judges with ermine dragging in the mud
And spotted here and there with guiltless blood;
Gold-greedy legislators jingling bribes;
Kept editors and sycophantic scribes;
Liars in swarms and plunderers in tribes;
They fade away before the night's advance,
And fancy figures thee a devil's lance
Gleaming portentous through the misty shade,
While ghosts of murdered virtues shriek about my blade!

A Study In Gray
I step from the door with a shiver
(This fog is uncommonly cold)
And ask myself: What did I give her?
The maiden a trifle gone-old,
With the head of gray hair that was gold.
Ah, well, I suppose 'twas a dollar,
And doubtless the change is correct,
Though it's odd that it seems so much smaller
Than what I'd a right to expect.
But you pay when you dine, I reflect.
So I walk up the street - 'twas a saunter
A score of years back, when I strolled
From this door; and our talk was all banter
Those days when her hair was of gold,
And the sea-fog less searching and cold.
I button my coat (for I'm shaken,
And fevered a trifle, and flushed
With the wine that I ought to have taken,)
Time was, at this coat I'd have blushed,
Though truly, 'tis cleverly brushed.
A score? Why, that isn't so very
Much time to have lost from a life.
There's reason enough to be merry:
I've not fallen down in the strife,
But marched with the drum and the fife.
If Hope, when she lured me and beckoned,
Had pushed at my shoulders instead,
And Fame, on whose favors I reckoned,
Had laureled the worthiest head,
I could garland the years that are dead.
Believe me, I've held my own, mostly
Through all of this wild masquerade;
But somehow the fog is more ghostly

To-night, and the skies are more grayed,
Like the locks of the restaurant maid.
If ever I'd fainted and faltered
I'd fancy this did but appear;
But the climate, I'm certain, has altered
Grown colder and more austere
Than it was in that earlier year.
The lights, too, are strangely unsteady,
That lead from the street to the quay.
I think they'll go out - and I'm ready
To follow. Out there in the sea
The fog-bell is calling to me.

A Vision Of Climate
I dreamed that I was poor and sick and sad,
Broken in hope and weary of my life;
My ventures all miscarrying - naught had
For all my labor in the heat and strife.
And in my heart some certain thoughts were rife
Of an unsummoned exit. As I lay
Considering my bitter state, I cried:
'Alas! that hither I did ever stray.
Better in some fair country to have died
Than live in such a land, where Fortune never
(Unless he be successful) crowns Endeavor.'
Then, even as I lamented, lo! there came
A troop of Presences - I knew not whence
Nor what they were: thought cannot rightly name
What's known through spiritual evidence,
Reported not by gross material sense.
'Why come ye here?' I seemed to cry (though naught
My sleeping tongue did utter) to the first
'What are ye? with what woful message fraught?
Ye have a ghastly look, as ye had burst
Some sepulcher in memory. Weird creatures,
I'm sure I'd know you if ye had but features.'
Some subtle organ noted the reply
(Inaudible to ear of flesh the tone):
'The Finest Climate in the World am I,
From Siskiyou to San Diego known
From the Sierra to the sea. The zone
Called semi-tropical I've pulled about
And placed it where it does most good, I trust.
I shake my never-failing bounty out
Alike upon the just and the unjust.'
'That's very true,' said I, 'but when 'tis shaken
My share by the unjust is ever taken.'
'Permit me,' it resumed, 'now to present
My eldest son, the Champagne Atmosphere,

And others to rebuke your discontent
The Mammoth Squash, Strawberry All the Year,
The fair No Lightning-flashing only here
The Wholesome Earthquake and Italian Sky,
With its Unstriking Sun; and last, not least,
The Compos Mentis Dog. Now, ingrate, try
To bring a better stomach to the feast:
When Nature makes a dance and pays the piper,
To be unhappy is to be a viper!'
'Why, yet,' said I, 'with all your blessings fine
(And Heaven forbid that I should speak them ill)
I yet am poor and sick and sad. Ye shine
With more of splendor than of heat: for still,
Although my will is warm, my bones are chill.'
'Then warm you with enthusiasm's blaze
Fortune waits not on toil,' they cried; 'O then
Join the wild chorus clamoring our praise
Throw up your beaver and throw down you pen!'
'Begone!' I shouted. They bewent, a-smirking,
And I, awakening, fell straight a-working.

A Vision Of Doom
I stood upon a hill. The setting sun
Was crimson with a curse and a portent,
And scarce his angry ray lit up the land
That lay below, whose lurid gloom appeared
Freaked with a moving mist, which, reeking up
From dim tarns hateful with some horrid ban,
Took shapes forbidden and without a name.
Gigantic night-birds, rising from the reeds
With cries discordant, startled all the air,
And bodiless voices babbled in the gloom
The ghosts of blasphemies long ages stilled,
And shrieks of women, and men's curses. All
These visible shapes, and sounds no mortal ear
Had ever heard, some spiritual sense
Interpreted, though brokenly; for I
Was haunted by a consciousness of crime,
Some giant guilt, but whose I knew not. All
These things malign, by sight and sound revealed,
Were sin begotten; that I knew no more
And that but dimly, as in dreadful dreams
The sleepy senses babble to the brain
Imperfect witness. As I stood a voice,
But whence it came I knew not, cried aloud
Some words to me in a forgotten tongue,
Yet straight I knew me for a ghost forlorn,
Returned from the illimited inane.
Again, but in a language that I knew,

As in reply to something which in me
Had shaped itself a thought, but found no words,
It spake from the dread mystery about:
'Immortal shadow of a mortal soul
That perished with eternity, attend.
What thou beholdest is as void as thou:
The shadow of a poet's dream - himself
As thou, his soul as thine, long dead,
But not like thine outlasted by its shade.
His dreams alone survive eternity
As pictures in the unsubstantial void.
Excepting thee and me (and we because
The poet wove us in his thought) remains
Of nature and the universe no part
Or vestige but the poet's dreams. This dread,
Unspeakable land about thy feet, with all
Its desolation and its terrors - lo!
'T is but a phantom world. So long ago
That God and all the angels since have died
That poet lived - yourself long dead - his mind
Filled with the light of a prophetic fire,
And standing by the Western sea, above
The youngest, fairest city in the world,
Named in another tongue than his for one
Ensainted, saw its populous domain
Plague-smitten with a nameless shame. For there
Red-handed murder rioted; and there
The people gathered gold, nor cared to loose
The assassin's fingers from the victim's throat,
But said, each in his vile pursuit engrossed:
'Am I my brother's keeper? Let the Law
Look to the matter.' But the Law did not.
And there, O pitiful! the babe was slain
Within its mother's breast and the same grave
Held babe and mother; and the people smiled,
Still gathering gold, and said: 'The Law, the Law,'
Then the great poet, touched upon the lips
With a live coal from Truth's high altar, raised
His arms to heaven and sang a song of doom
Sang of the time to be, when God should lean
Indignant from the Throne and lift his hand,
And that foul city be no more! a tale,
A dream, a desolation and a curse!
No vestige of its glory should survive
In fact or memory: its people dead,
Its site forgotten, and its very name Disputed.'
'Was the prophecy fulfilled?'
The sullen disc of the declining sun
Was crimson with a curse and a portent,
And scarce his angry ray lit up the land
That lay below, whose lurid gloom appeared

Freaked with a moving mist, which, reeking up
From dim tarns hateful with a horrid ban,
Took shapes forbidden and without a name.
Gigantic night-birds, rising from the reeds
With cries discordant, startled all the air,
And bodiless voices babbled in the gloom.
But not to me came any voice again;
And, covering my face with thin, dead hands,
I wept, and woke, and cried aloud to God!

A Vision Of Resurrection
I had a dream. The habitable earth
Its continents and islands, all were bare
Of cities and of forests. Naught remained
Of its old aspect, and I only knew
(As men know things in dreams, unknowing how)
That this was earth and that all men were dead.
On every side I saw the barren land,
Even to the distant sky's inclosing blue,
Thick-pitted all with graves; and all the graves
Save one were open - not as newly dug,
But rather as by some internal force
Riven for egress. Tombs of stone were split
And wide agape, and in their iron decay
The massive mausoleums stood in halves.
With mildewed linen all the ground was white.
Discarded shrouds upon memorial stones
Hung without motion in the soulless air.
While greatly marveling how this should be
I heard, or fancied that I heard, a voice,
Low like an angel's, delicately strong,
And sweet as music.
'Spirit,' it said, 'behold
The burial place of universal Man!
A million years have rolled away since here
His sheeted multitudes (save only some
Whose dark misdeeds required a separate
And individual arraignment) rose
To judgment at the trumpet's summoning
And passed into the sky for their award,
Leaving behind these perishable things
Which yet, preserved by miracle, endure
Till all are up. Then they and all of earth,
Rock-hearted mountain and storm-breasted sea,
River and wilderness and sites of dead
And vanished capitals of men, shall spring
To flame, and naught shall be for evermore!
When all are risen that wonder will occur.
'Twas but ten centuries ago the last

But one came forth - a soul so black with sin,
Against whose name so many crimes were set
That only now his trial is at end. But one remains.'
Straight, as the voice was stilled
That single rounded mound cracked lengthliwise
And one came forth in grave-clothes. For a space
He stood and gazed about him with a smile
Superior; then laying off his shroud
Disclosed his two attenuated legs
Which, like parentheses, bent outwardly
As by the weight of saintliness above,
And so sprang upward and was lost to view
Noting his headstone overthrown, I read:
'Sacred to memory of George K. Fitch,
Deacon and Editor - a holy man
Who fell asleep in Jesus, full of years
And blessedness. The dead in Christ rise first.'

A Voluptuary
Who's this that lispeth in the thickening throng
Which crowds to claim distinction in my song?
Fresh from 'the palms and temples of the South,'
The mixed aromas quarrel in his mouth:
Of orange blossoms this the lingering gale,
And that the odor of a spicy tale.
Sir, in thy pleasure-dome down by the sea
(No finer one did Kubla Khan decree)
Where, Master of the Revels, thou dost stand
With joys and mysteries on either hand,
Dost keep a poet to report the rites
And sing the tale of those Elysian nights?
Faith, sir, I'd like the place if not too young.
I'm no great bard, but - I can hold my tongue.

A Warning
Cried Age to Youth: 'Abate your speed!
The distance hither's brief indeed.'
But Youth pressed on without delay
The shout had reached but half the way

A Welcome
Because you call yourself Knights Templar, and
There's neither Knight nor Temple in the land,
Because you thus by vain pretense degrade
To paltry purposes traditions grand,

Because to cheat the ignorant you say
The thing that's not, elated still to sway
The crass credulity of gaping fools
And women by fantastical display,
Because no sacred fires did ever warm
Your hearts, high knightly service to perform
A woman's breast or coffer of a man
The only citadel you dare to storm,
Because while railing still at lord and peer,
At pomp and fuss-and-feathers while you jeer,
Each member of your order tries to graft
A peacock's tail upon his barren rear,
Because that all these things are thus and so,
I bid you welcome to our city. Lo!
You're free to come, and free to stay, and free
As soon as it shall please you, sirs - to go.

A Wet Season

The rain is fierce, it flogs the earth,
And man's in danger.
O that my mother at my birth
Had borne a stranger!
The flooded ground is all around.
The depth uncommon.
How blest I'd be if only she
Had borne a salmon.
If still denied the solar glow
'T were bliss ecstatic
To be amphibious - but O,
To be aquatic!
We're worms, men say, o' the dust, and they
That faith are firm of.
O, then, be just: show me some dust
To be a worm of.
The pines are chanting overhead
A psalm uncheering.
It's O, to have been for ages dead
And hard of hearing!
Restore, ye Pow'rs, the last bright hours
The dial reckoned;
'Twas in the time of Egypt's prime
Rameses II.

A Whipper-In

Dudley, great placeman, man of mark and note,
Worthy of honor from a feeble pen
Blunted in service of all true, good men,

You serve the Lord in courses, table d'hote:
Au, naturel, as well as a la Nick
'Eat and be thankful, though it make you sick.'
O, truly pious caterer, forbear
To push the Saviour and Him crucified
(Brochette you'd call it) into their inside
Who're all unused to such ambrosial fare.
The stomach of the soul makes quick revulsion
Of aught that it has taken on compulsion.
I search the Scriptures, but I do not find
That e'er the Spirit beats with angry wings
For entrance to the heart, but sits and sings
To charm away the scruples of the mind.
It says: 'Receive me, please; I'll not compel'
Though if you don't you will go straight to Hell!
Well, that's compulsion, you will say. 'T is true:
We cower timidly beneath the rod
Lifted in menace by an angry God,
But won't endure it from an ape like you.
Detested simian with thumb prehensile,
Switch me and I would brain you with my pencil!
Face you the Throne, nor dare to turn your back
On its transplendency to flog some wight
Who gropes and stumbles in the infernal night
Your ugly shadow lays along his track.
O, Thou who from the Temple scourged the sin,
Behold what rascals try to scourge it in!

A Word To The Unwise

Charles Main, of Main & Winchester, attend
With friendly ear the chit-chat of a friend
Who knows you not, yet knows that you and he
Travel two roads that have a common end.
We journey forward through the time allowed,
I humbly bending, you erect and proud.
Our heads alike will stable soon the worm
The one that's lifted, and the one that's bowed.
You in your mausoleum shall repose,
I where it pleases Him who sleep bestows;
What matter whether one so little worth
Shall stain the marble or shall feed the rose?
Charles Main, I had a friend who died one day.
A metal casket held his honored clay.
Of cyclopean architecture stood
The splendid vault where he was laid away.
A dozen years, and lo! the roots of grass
Had burst asunder all the joints; the brass,
The gilded ornaments, the carven stones
Lay tumbled all together in a mass.

A dozen years! That taxes your belief.
Make it a thousand if the time's too brief.
'Twill be the same to you; when you are dead
You cannot even count your days of grief.
Suppose a pompous monument you raise
Till on its peak the solar splendor blaze
While yet about its base the night is black;
But will it give your glory length of days?
Say, when beneath your rubbish has been thrown,
Some rogue to reputation all unknown
Men's backs being turned - should lift his thieving hand,
Efface your name and substitute his own.
Whose then would be the monument? To whom
Would be the fame? Forgotten in your gloom,
Your very name forgotten - ah, my friend,
The name is all that's rescued by the tomb.
For memory of worth and work we go
To other records than a stone can show.
These lacking, naught remains; with these
The stone is needless for the world will know.
Then build your mausoleum if you must,
And creep into it with a perfect trust;
But in the twinkling of an eye the plow
Shall pass without obstruction through your dust.
Another movement of the pendulum,
And, lo! the desert haunting wolf shall come,
And, seated on the spot, shall howl by night
O'er rotting cities, desolate and dumb.

A Wreath Of Immortelles
LORING PICKERING
(After Pope)
Here rests a writer, great but not immense,
Born destitute of feeling and of sense.
No power he but o'er his brain desired
How not to suffer it to be inspired.
Ideas unto him were all unknown,
Proud of the words which, only, were his own.
So unreflecting, so confused his mind,
Torpid in error, indolently blind,
A fever Heaven, to quicken him, applied,
But, rather than revive, the sluggard died.

A WATER-PIRATE
Pause, stranger whence you lightly tread
Bill Carr's immoral part has fled.
For him no heart of woman burned,
But all the rivers' heads he turned.
Alas! he now lifts up his eyes

In torment and for water cries,
Entreating that he may procure
One dropp to cool his parched McClure!

C.P. BERRY
Here's crowbait! ravens, too, and daws
Flock hither to advance their caws,
And, with a sudden courage armed,
Devour the foe who once alarmed
In life and death a fair deceit:
Nor strong to harm nor good to eat.
King bogey of the scarecrow host,
When known the least affrighting most,
Though light his hand (his mind was dark)
He left on earth a straw Berry mark.

THE REV. JOSEPH
He preached that sickness he could floor
By prayer and by commanding;
When sick himself he sent for four
Physicians in good standing.
He was struck dead despite their care,
For, fearing their dissension,
He secretly put up a prayer,
Thus drawing God's attention.

Cynic perforce from studying mankind
In the false volume of his single mind,
He damned his fellows for his own unworth,
And, bad himself, thought nothing good on earth.
Yet, still so judging and so erring still,
Observing well, but understanding ill,
His learning all was got by dint of sight,
And what he learned by day he lost by night.
When hired to flatter he would never cease
Till those who'd paid for praises paid for peace.
Not wholly miser and but half a knave,
He yearned to squander but he lived to save,
And did not, for he could not, cheat the grave.
Hic jacet Pixley, scribe and muleteer:
Step lightly, stranger, anywhere but here.

McAllister, of talents rich and rare,
Lies at this spot at finish of his race.
Alike to him if it is here or there:
The one spot that he cared for was the ace.

Here lies Joseph Redding, who gave us the catfish.
He dined upon every fish except that fish.
'Twas touching to hear him expounding his fad
With a heart full of zeal and a mouth full of shad.

The catfish miaowed with unspeakable woe
When Death, the lone fisherman, landed their Jo.

Judge Sawyer, whom in vain the people tried
To push from power, here is laid aside.
Death only from the bench could ever start
The sluggish load of his immortal part.

John Irish went, one luckless day,
To loaf and fish at San Jose.
He got no loaf, he got no fish:
They brained him with an empty dish!
They laid him in this place asleep
O come, ye crocodiles, and weep.

In Sacramento City here
This wooden monument we rear
In memory of Dr. May,
Whose smile even Death could not allay.
He's buried, Heaven alone knows where,
And only the hyenas care;
This May-pole merely marks the spot
Where, ere the wretch began to rot,
Fame's trumpet, with its brazen bray,
Bawled; 'Who (and why) was Dr. May?'

Dennis Spencer's mortal coil
Here is laid away to spoil
Great riparian, who said
Not a stream should leave its bed.
Now his soul would like a river
Turned upon its parching liver.

For those this mausoleum is erected
Who Stanford to the Upper House elected.
Their luck is less or their promotion slower,
For, dead, they were elected to the Lower.

Beneath this stone lies Reuben Lloyd,
Of breath deprived, of sense devoid.
The Templars' Captain-General, he
So formidable seemed to be,
That had he not been on his back
Death ne'er had ventured to attack.

Here lies Barnes in all his glory
Master he of oratOry.
When he died the people weeping,
(For they thought him only sleeping)
Cried: 'Although he now is quiet
And his tongue is not a riot,

Soon, the spell that binds him breaking,
He a motion will be making.
Then, alas, he'll rise and speak
In support of it a week.'

Rash mortal! stay thy feet and look around
This vacant tomb as yet is holy ground;
But soon, alas! Jim Fair will occupy
These premises then, holiness, good-bye!

Here Salomon's body reposes;
Bring roses, ye rebels, bring roses.
Set all of your drumsticks a-rolling,
Discretion and Valor extrolling:
Discretion he always retreated
And Valor the dead he defeated.
Brings roses, ye loyal, bring roses:
As patriot here he re-poses.

When Waterman ended his bright career
He left his wet name to history here.
To carry it with him he did not care:
'Twould tantalize spirits of statesmen There.

Here lie the remains of Fred Emerson Brooks,
A poet, as every one knew by his looks
Who hadn't unluckily met with his books.
On civic occasions he sprang to the fore
With poems consisting of stanzas three score.
The men whom they deafened enjoyed them the more.

Of reason his fantasy knew not the check:
All forms of inharmony came at his beck.
The weight of his ignorance fractured his neck.
In this peaceful spot, so the grave-diggers say,
With pen, ink and paper they laid him away
The Poet-elect of the Judgment Day.

George Perry here lies stiff and stark,
With stone at foot and stone at head.
His heart was dark, his mind was dark
'Ignorant ass!' the people said.
Not ignorant but skilled, alas,
In all the secrets of his trade:
He knew more ways to be an ass
Than any ass that ever brayed.

Here lies the last of Deacon Fitch,
Whose business was to melt the pitch.
Convenient to this sacred spot

Lies Sammy, who applied it, hot.
'Tis hard so much alike they smell
One's grave from t'other's grave to tell,
But when his tomb the Deacon's burst
(Of two he'll always be the first)
He'll see by studying the stones
That he's obtained his proper bones,
Then, seeking Sammy's vault, unlock it,
And put that person in his pocket.

Beneath this stone O'Donnell's tongue's at rest
Our noses by his spirit still addressed.
Living or dead, he's equally Satanic
His noise a terror and his smell a panic.

When Gabriel blows a dreadful blast
And swears that Time's forever past,
Days, weeks, months, years all one at last,
Then Asa Fiske, laid here, distressed,
Will beat (and skin his hand) his breast:
There'll be no rate of interest!

Step lightly, stranger: here Jerome B. Cox
Is for the second time in a bad box.
He killed a man the labor party rose
And showed him by its love how killing goes.

When Vrooman here lay down to sleep,
The other dead awoke to weep.
'Since he no longer lives,' they said
'Small honor comes of being dead.'

Here Porter Ashe is laid to rest
Green grows the grass upon his breast.
This patron of the turf, I vow,
Ne'er served it half so well as now.

Like a cold fish escaping from its tank,
Hence fled the soul of Joe Russel, crank.
He cried: 'Cold water!' roaring like a beast.
'Twas thrown upon him and the music ceased.

Here Estee rests. He shook a basket,
When, like a jewel from its casket,
Fell Felton out. Said Estee, shouting
With mirth; 'I've given you an outing.'
Then told him to go back. He wouldn't.
Then tried to put him back. He couldn't.
So Estee died (his blood congealing
In Felton's growing shadow) squealing.

Mourn here for one Bruner, called Elwood.
He doesn't - he never did - smell good
To noses of critics and scholars.
If now he'd an office to sell could
He sell it? O, no where (in Hell) could
He find a cool four hundred dollars?

Here Stanford lies, who thought it odd
That he should go to meet his God.
He looked, until his eyes grew dim,
For God to hasten to meet him.

A Wreath Of Immortelles
Judge Sawyer, whom in vain the people tried
To push from power, here is laid aside.
Death only from the bench could ever start
The sluggish load of his immortal part.

For those this mausoleum is erected
Who Stanford to the Upper House elected.
Their luck is less or their promotion slower,
For, dead, they were elected to the Lower.

Rash mortal! stay thy feet and look around
This vacant tomb as yet is holy ground;
But soon, alas! Jim Fair will occupy
These premises then, holiness, good-bye!

George Perry here lies stiff and stark,
With stone at foot and stone at head.
His heart was dark, his mind was dark
'Ignorant ass!' the people said.
Not ignorant but skilled, alas,
In all the secrets of his trade:
He knew more ways to be an ass
Than any ass that ever brayed.

A Year's Casualties
Slain as they lay by the secret, slow,
Pitiless hand of an unseen foe,
Two score thousand old soldiers have crossed
The river to join the loved and lost.
In the space of a year their spirits fled,
Silent and white, to the camp of the dead.
One after one, they fall asleep
And the pension agents awake to weep,
And orphaned statesmen are loud in their wail

As the souls flit by on the evening gale.
O Father of Battles, pray give us release
From the horrors of peace, the horrors of peace!

Accepted

Charles Shortridge once to St. Peter came.
'Down!' cried the saint with his face aflame;
''Tis writ that every hardy liar
Shall dwell forever and ever in fire!'
'That's what I said the night that I died,'
The sinner, turning away, replied.
'What! you said that?' cried the saint 'what! what!
You said 'twas so writ? Then, faith, 'tis not!
I'm a devil at quoting, but I begin
To fail in my memory. Pray walk in.'

Ad Cattonum

I know not, Mr. Catton, who you are,
Nor very clearly why; but you go far
To show that you are many things beside
A Chilean Consul with a tempting hide;
But what they are I hardly could explain
Without afflicting you with mental pain.
Your name (gods! what a name the muse to woo
Suggesting cats, and hinting kittens, too!)
Points to an origin perhaps Maltese,
Perhaps Angoran where the wicked cease
From fiddling, and the animals that grow
The strings that groan to the tormenting bow
Live undespoiled of their insides, resigned
To give their name and nature to mankind.
With Chilean birth your name but poorly tallies;
The test is - Did you ever sell tamales?
It matters very little, though, my boy,
If you're from Chile or from Illinois;
You can't, because you serve a foreign land,
Spit with impunity on ours, expand,
Cock-turkeywise, and strut with blind conceit,
All heedless of the hearts beneath your feet,
Fling falsehoods as a sower scatters grain
And, for security, invoke disdain.
Sir, there are laws that men of sense observe,
No matter whence they come nor whom they serve
The laws of courtesy; and these forbid
You to malign, as recently you did,
As servant of another State, a State
Wherein your duties all are concentrate;

Branding its Ministers as rogues in short,
Inviting cuffs as suitable retort.
Chileno or American, 'tis one
Of any land a citizen, or none
If like a new Thersites here you rail,
Loading with libels every western gale,
You'll feel the cudgel on your scurvy hump
Impinging with a salutary thump.
'Twill make you civil or 'twill make you jump!

Ad Moodium
Tut! Moody, do not try to show
To gentlemen and ladies
That if they have not 'Faith,' they'll go
Headlong to Hades.
Faith is belief; and how can I
Have that by being willing?
This dime I cannot, though I try,
Believe a shilling.
Perhaps you can. If so, pray do
Believe you own it, also.
But what seems evidence to you
I may not call so.
Heaven knows I'd like the Faith to think
This little vessel's contents
Are liquid gold. I see 'tis ink
For writing nonsense.
Minds prone to Faith, however, may
Come now and then to sorrow:
They put their trust in truth to-day,
In lies to-morrow.
No doubt the happiness is great
To think as one would wish to;
But not to swallow every bait,
As certain fish do.
To think a snake a cord, I hope,
Would bolden and delight me;
But some day I might think a rope
Would chase and bite me.
'Curst Reason! Faith forever blest!'
You're crying all the season.
Well, who decides that Faith is best?
Why, Mr. Reason.
He's right or wrong; he answers you
According to your folly,
And says what you have taught him to,
Like any polly.

Adair Welcker, Poet

The Swan of Avon died the Swan
Of Sacramento'll soon be gone;
And when his death-song he shall coo,
Stand back, or it will kill you too.

Again

Well, I've met her again at the Mission.
She'd told me to see her no more;
It was not a command a petition;
I'd granted it once before.
Yes, granted it, hoping she'd write me.
Repenting her virtuous freak
Subdued myself daily and nightly
For the better part of a week.
And then ('twas my duty to spare her
The shame of recalling me) I
Just sought her again to prepare her
For an everlasting good-bye.
O, that evening of bliss shall I ever
Forget it? with Shakespeare and Poe!
She said, when 'twas ended: 'You're never
To see me again. And now go.'
As we parted with kisses 'twas human
And natural for me to smile
As I thought, 'She's in love, and a woman:
She'll send for me after a while.'
But she didn't; and so well, the Mission
Is fine, picturesque and gray;
It's an excellent place for contrition
And sometimes she passes that way.
That's how it occurred that I met her,
And that's ah there is to tell
Except that I'd like to forget her
Calm way of remarking: 'I'm well.'
It was hardly worth while, all this keying
My soul to such tensions and stirs
To learn that her food was agreeing
With that little stomach of hers.

Alone

In contact, lo! the flint and steel,
By sharp and flame, the thought reveal
That he the metal, she the stone,
Had cherished secretly alone.

An Actor

Some one ('tis hardly new) has oddly said
The color of a trumpet's blare is red;
And Joseph Emmett thinks the crimson shame
On woman's cheek a trumpet-note of fame.
The more the red storm rises round her nose
The more her eyes averted seek her toes,
He fancies all the louder he can hear
The tube resounding in his spacious ear,
And, all his varied talents to exert,
Darkens his dullness to display his dirt.
And when the gallery's indecent crowd,
And gentlemen below, with hisses loud,
In hot contention (these his art to crown,
And those his naked nastiness to drown)
Make such a din that cheeks erewhile aflame
Grow white and in their fear forget their shame,
With impudence imperial, sublime,
Unmoved, the patient actor bides his time,
Till storm and counter-storm are both allayed,
Like donkeys, each by t'other one outbrayed.
When all the place is silent as a mouse
One slow, suggestive gesture clears the house!

An Alibi

A famous journalist, who long
Had told the great unheaded throng
Whate'er they thought, by day or night.
Was true as Holy Writ, and right,
Was caught in, well, on second thought,
It is enough that he was caught,
And being thrown in jail became
The fuel of a public flame.
'Vox populi vox Dei,' said
The jailer. Inxling bent his head
Without remark: that motto good
In bold-faced type had always stood
Above the columns where his pen
Had rioted in praise of men
And all they said provided he
Was sure they mostly did agree.
Meanwhile a sharp and bitter strife
To take, or save, the culprit's life
Or liberty (which, I suppose,
Was much the same to him) arose
Outside. The journal that his pen
Adorned denounced his crime but then

Its editor in secret tried
To have the indictment set aside.
The opposition papers swore
His father was a rogue before,
And all his wife's relations were
Like him and similar to her.
They begged their readers to subscribe
A dollar each to make a bribe
That any Judge would feel was large
Enough to prove the gravest charge
Unless, it might be, the defense
Put up superior evidence.
The law's traditional delay
Was all too short: the trial day
Dawned red and menacing. The Judge
Sat on the Bench and wouldn't budge,
And all the motions counsel made
Could not move him and there he stayed.
'The case must now proceed,' he said,
'While I am just in heart and head,
It happens-as, indeed, it ought
Both sides with equal sums have bought
My favor: I can try the cause
Impartially.' (Prolonged applause.)
The prisoner was now arraigned
And said that he was greatly pained
To be suspected he, whose pen
Had charged so many other men
With crimes and misdemeanors! 'Why,'
He said, a tear in either eye,
'If men who live by crying out
'Stop thief!' are not themselves from doubt
Of their integrity exempt,
Let all forego the vain attempt
To make a reputation! Sir,
I'm innocent, and I demur.'
Whereat a thousand voices cried
Amain he manifestly lied
Vox populi as loudly roared
As bull by picadores gored,
In his own coin receiving pay
To make a Spanish holiday.
The jury, twelve good men and true
Were then sworn in to see it through,
And each made solemn oath that he
As any babe unborn was free
From prejudice, opinion, thought,
Respectability, brains aught
That could disqualify; and some
Explained that they were deaf and dumb.
A better twelve, his Honor said,

Was rare, except among the dead.
The witnesses were called and sworn.
The tales they told made angels mourn,
And the Good Book they'd kissed became
Red with the consciousness of shame.
Whenever one of them approached
The truth, 'That witness wasn't coached,
Your Honor!' cried the lawyers both.
'Strike out his testimony,' quoth
The learned judge: 'This Court denies
Its ear to stories which surprise.
I hold that witnesses exempt
From coaching all are in contempt.'
Both Prosecution and Defense
Applauded the judicial sense,
And the spectators all averred
Such wisdom they had never heard:
'Twas plain the prisoner would be
Found guilty in the first degree.
Meanwhile that wight's pale cheek confessed
The nameless terrors in his breast.
He felt remorseful, too, because
He wasn't half they said he was.
'If I'd been such a rogue,' he mused
On opportunities unused,
'I might have easily become
As wealthy as Methusalum.'

This journalist adorned, alas,
The middle, not the Bible, class.
With equal skill the lawyers' pleas
Attested their divided fees.
Each gave the other one the lie,
Then helped him frame a sharp reply.
Good Lord! it was a bitter fight,
And lasted all the day and night.
When once or oftener the roar
Had silenced the judicial snore
The speaker suffered for the sport
By fining for contempt of court.
Twelve jurors' noses good and true
Unceasing sang the trial through,
And even vox populi was spent
In rattles through a nasal vent.
Clerk, bailiff, constables and all
Heard Morpheus sound the trumpet call
To arms - his arms - and all fell in
Save counsel for the Man of Sin.
That thaumaturgist stood and swayed
The wand their faculties obeyed
That magic wand which, like a flame.

Leapt, wavered, quivered and became
A wonder worker known among
The ignoble vulgar as a Tongue.
How long, O Lord, how long my verse
Runs on for better or for worse
In meter which o'ermasters me,
Octosyllabically free!
A meter which, the poets say,
No power of restraint can stay;
A hard mouthed meter, suited well
To him who, having naught to tell,
Must hold attention as a trout
Is held, by paying out and out
The slender line which else would break
Should one attempt the fish to take.
Thus tavern guides who've naught to show
But some adjacent curio
By devious trails their patrons lead
And make them think 't is far indeed.
Where was I?
While the lawyer talked
The rogue took up his feet and walked:
While all about him, roaring, slept,
Into the street he calmly stepped.
In very truth, the man who thought
The people's voice from heaven had caught
God's inspiration took a change
Of venue - it was passing strange!
Straight to his editor he went
And that ingenious person sent
A Negro to impersonate
The fugitive. In adequate
Disguise he took his vacant place
And buried in his arms his face.
When all was done the lawyer stopped
And silence like a bombshell dropped
Upon the Court: judge, jury, all
Within that venerable hall
(Except the deaf and dumb, indeed,
And one or two whom death had freed)
Awoke and tried to look as though
Slumber was all they did not know.
And now that tireless lawyer-man
Took breath, and then again began:
'Your Honor, if you did attend
To what I've urged (my learned friend
Nodded concurrence) to support
The motion I have made, this court
May soon adjourn. With your assent
I've shown abundant precedent
For introducing now, though late,

New evidence to exculpate
My client. So, if you'll allow,
I'll prove an alibi!' 'What? how?'
Stammered the judge. 'Well, yes, I can't
Deny your showing, and I grant
The motion. Do I understand
You undertake to prove, good land!
That when the crime - you mean to show
Your client wasn't there?' 'O, no,
I cannot quite do that, I find:
My alibi's another kind
Of alibi, I'll make it clear,
Your Honor, that he isn't here.'
The Darky here upreared his head,
Tranquillity affrighted fled
And consternation reigned instead!

An Anarchist

False to his art and to the high command
God laid upon him, Markham's rebel hand
Beats all in vain the harp he touched before:
It yields a jingle and it yields no more.
No more the strings beneath his finger-tips
Sing harmonies divine. No more his lips,
Touched with a living coal from sacred fires,
Lead the sweet chorus of the golden wires.
The voice is raucous and the phrases squeak;
They labor, they complain, they sweat, they reek!
The more the wayward, disobedient song
Errs from the right to celebrate the wrong,
More diligently still the singer strums,
To drown the horrid sound, with all his thumbs.
Gods, what a spectacle! The angels lean
Out of high Heaven to view the sorry scene,
And Israfel, 'whose heart-strings are a lute,'
Though now compassion makes their music mute,
Among the weeping company appears,
Pearls in his eyes and cotton in his ears.

An Apologue

A traveler observed one day
A loaded fruit-tree by the way.
And reining in his horse exclaimed:
'The man is greatly to be blamed
Who, careless of good morals, leaves
Temptation in the way of thieves.
Now lest some villain pass this way

And by this fruit be led astray
To bag it, I will kindly pack
It snugly in my saddle-sack.'
He did so; then that Salt o' the Earth
Rode on, rejoicing in his worth.

An Art Critic

Ira P. Rankin, you've a nasal name
I'll sound it through 'the speaking trump of fame,'
And wondering nations, hearing from afar
The brazen twang of its resounding jar,
Shall say: 'These bards are an uncommon class
They blow their noses with a tube of brass!'
Rankin! ye gods! if Influenza pick
Our names at christening, and such names stick,
Let's all be born when summer suns withstand
Her prevalence and chase her from the land,
And healing breezes generously help
To shield from death each ailing human whelp!
'What's in a name?' There's much at least in yours
That the pained ear unwillingly endures,
And much to make the suffering soul, I fear,
Envy the lesser anguish of the ear.
So you object to Cytherea! Do,
The picture was not painted, sir, for you!
Your mind to gratify and taste address,
The masking dove had been a dove the less.
Provincial censor! all untaught in art,
With mind indecent and indecent heart,
Do you not know, nay, why should I explain?
Instruction, argument alike were vain
I'll show you reasons when you show me brain.

An Augury

Upon my desk a single spray,
With starry blossoms fraught.
I write in many an idle way,
Thinking one serious thought.
'O flowers, a fine Greek name ye bear,
And with a fine Greek grace.'
Be still, O heart, that turns to share
The sunshine of a face.
'Have ye no messages, no brief,
Still sign: 'Despair', or 'Hope'?'
A sudden stir of stem and leaf
A breath of heliotrope!

An Average
I ne'er could be entirely fond
Of any maiden who's a blonde,
And no brunette that e'er I saw
Had charms my heart's whole
warmth to draw.
Yet sure no girl was ever made
Just half of light and half of shade.
And so, this happy mean to get,
I love a blonde and a brunette.

An Enemy To Law And Order
A is defrauded of his land by B,
Who's driven from the premises by C.
D buys the place with coin of plundered E.
'That A's an Anarchist!' says F to G.

An Epitaph
Hangman's hands laid in this tomb an
Imp of Satan's getting, whom an
Ancient legend says that woman
Never bore, he owed his birth
To Sin herself. From Hell to Earth
She brought the brat in secret state
And laid him at the Golden gate,
And they named him Henry Vrooman.
While with mortals here he stayed,
His father frequently he played.
Raised his birth-place and in other
Playful ways begot his mother.

An Epitaph
Here lies Greer Harrison, a well cracked louse
So small a tenant of so big a house!
He joyed in fighting with his eyes (his fist
Prudently pendent from a peaceful wrist)
And loved to loll on the Parnassian mount,
His pen to suck and all his thumbs to count,
What poetry he'd written but for lack
Of skill, when he had counted, to count back!
Alas, no more he'll climb the sacred steep
To wake the lyre and put the world to sleep!
To his rapt lip his soul no longer springs

And like a jaybird from a knot-hole sings.
No more the clubmen, pickled with his wine,
Spread wide their ears and hiccough 'That's divine!'
The genius of his purse no longer draws
The pleasing thunders of a paid applause.
All silent now, nor sound nor sense remains,
Though riddances of worms improve his brains.
All his no talents to the earth revert,
And Fame concludes the record: 'Dirt to dirt!'

An Example

They were two deaf mutes, and they loved and they
Resolved to be groom and bride;
And they listened to nothing that any could say,
Nor ever a word replied.
From wedlock when warned by the married men,
Maintain an invincible mind:
Be deaf and dumb until wedded and then
Be deaf and dumb and blind.

An 'Exhibit'

Goldenson hanged! Well, Heaven forbid
That I should smile above him:
Though truth to tell, I never did
Exactly love him.
It can't be wrong, though, to rejoice
That his unpleasing capers
Are ended. Silent is his voice
In all the papers.
No longer he's a show: no more,
Bear-like, his den he's walking.
No longer can he hold the floor
When I'd be talking.
The laws that govern jails are bad
If such displays are lawful.
The fate of the assassin's sad,
But ours is awful!
What! shall a wretch condemned to die
In shame upon the gibbet
Be set before the public eye
As an 'exhibit'?
His looks, his actions noted down,
His words if light or solemn,
And all this hawked about the town
So much a column?
The press, of course, will publish news
However it may get it;

But blast the sheriff who'll abuse
His powers to let it!
Nay, this is not ingratitude;
I'm no reporter, truly,
Nor yet an editor. I'm rude
Because unruly
Because I burn with shame and rage
Beyond my power of telling
To see assassins in a cage
And keepers yelling.
'Walk up! Walk up!' the showman cries:
'Observe the lion's poses,
His stormy mane, his glooming eyes.
His - hold your noses!'
How long, O Lord, shall Law and Right
Be mocked for gain or glory,
And angels weep as they recite
The shameful story?

An Exile
'Tis the census enumerator
A-singing all forlorn:
It's ho! for the tall potater,
And ho! for the clustered corn.
The whiffle-tree bends in the breeze and the fine
Large eggs are a-ripening on the vine.
'Some there must be to till the soil
And the widow's weeds keep down.
I wasn't cut out for rural toil
But they won't let me live in town!
They 're not so many by two or three,
As they think, but ah! they 're too many for me.'
Thus the census man, bowed down with care,
Warbled his wood-note high.
There was blood on his brow and blood in his hair,
But he had no blood in his eye.

An Explanation
'I never yet exactly could determine
Just how it is that the judicial ermine
Is kept so safely from predacious vermin.'
'It is not so, my friend: though in a garret
'Tis kept in camphor, and you often air it,
The vermin will get into it and wear it.'

An Idler

Who told Creed Haymond he was witty? who
Had nothing better in this world to do?
Could no greased pig's appeal to his embrace
Kindle his ardor for the friendly chase?
Did no dead dog upon a vacant lot,
Bloated and bald, or curdled in a clot,
Stir his compassion and inspire his arms
To hide from human eyes its faded charms?
If not to works of piety inclined,
Then recreation might have claimed his mind.
The harmless game that shows the feline greed
To cinch the shorts and make the market bleed
Is better sport than victimizing Creed;
And a far livelier satisfaction comes
Of knowing Simon, autocrat of thumbs.
If neither worthy work nor play command
This gentleman of leisure's heart and hand,
Then Mammon might his idle spirit lift
By hope of profit to some deed of thrift.
Is there no cheese to pare, no flint to skin,
No tin to mend, no glass to be put in,
No housewife worthy of a morning visit,
Her rags and sacks and bottles to solicit?
Lo! the blind sow's precarious pursuit
Of the aspiring oak's familiar fruit!
'Twould more advantage any man to steal
This easy victim's undefended meal
Than tell Creed Haymond he has wit, and so
Expose the state to his narcotic flow!

An Imposter

Must you, Carnegie, evermore explain
Your worth, and all the reasons give again
Why black and red are similarly white,
And you and God identically right?
Still must our ears without redress submit
To hear you play the solemn hypocrite
Walking in spirit some high moral level,
Raising at once his eye-balls and the devil?
Great King of Cant! if Nature had but made
Your mouth without a tongue I ne'er had prayed
To have an earless head. Since she did not,
Bear me, ye whirlwinds, to some favored spot
Some mountain pinnacle that sleeps in air
So delicately, mercifully rare
That when the fellow climbs that giddy hill,
As, for my sins, I know at last he will,
To utter twaddle in that void inane

His soundless organ he will play in vain.

An Inscription

A conqueror as provident as brave,
He robbed the cradle to supply the grave.
His reign laid quantities of human dust:
He fell upon the just and the unjust.

An Inscription

(For a Proposed Monument in Washington)
Erected to 'Boss' Shepherd by the dear
Good folk he lived and moved among in peace
Guarded on either hand by the police,
With soldiers in his front and in his rear.

An Inscription

(For A Statue Of Napoleon, At West Point)
A famous conqueror, in battle brave,
Who robbed the cradle to supply the grave.
His reign laid quantities of human dust:
He fell upon the just and the unjust.

An Interpretation

Now Lonergan appears upon the boards,
And Truth and Error sheathe their lingual swords.
No more in wordy warfare to engage,
The commentators bow before the stage,
And bookworms, militant for ages past,
Confess their equal foolishness at last,
Reread their Shakspeare in the newer light
And swear the meaning's obvious to sight.
For centuries the question has been hot:
Was Hamlet crazy, or was Hamlet not?
Now, Lonergan's illuminating art
Reveals the truth of the disputed 'part,'
And shows to all the critics of the earth
That Hamlet was an idiot from birth!

An Obituarian

Death-poet Pickering sat at his desk,
Wrapped in appropriate gloom;

His posture was pensive and picturesque,
Like a raven charming a tomb.
Enter a party a-drinking the cup
Of sorrow and likewise of woe:
'Some harrowing poetry, Mister, whack up,
All wrote in the key of O.
'For the angels has called my old woman hence
From the strife (where she fit mighty free).
It's a nickel a line? Condemn the expense!
For wealth is now little to me.'
The Bard of Mortality looked him through
In the piercingest sort of a way:
'It is much to me though it's little to you
I've taken a wife to-day.'
So he twisted the tail of his mental cow
And made her give down her flow.
The grief of that bard was long-winded, somehow
There was reams and reamses of woe.
The widower man which had buried his wife
Grew lily-like round each gill,
For she turned in her grave and came back to life
Then he cruel ignored the bill!
Then Sorrow she opened her gates a-wide,
As likewise did also Woe,
And the death-poet's song, as is heard inside,
Is sang in the key of O.

An Offer Of Marriage
Once I 'dipt into the future far as human eye could see,'
And saw it was not Sandow, nor John Sullivan, but she
The Emancipated Woman, who was weeping as she ran
Here and there for the discovery of Expurgated Man.
But the sun of Evolution ever rose and ever set,
And that tardiest of mortals hadn't evolved yet.
Hence the tears that she cascaded, hence the sighs that tore apart
All the tendinous connections of her indurated heart.
Cried Emancipated Woman, as she wearied of the search:
'In Advancing I have left myself distinctly in the lurch!
Seeking still a worthy partner, from the land of brutes and dudes
I have penetrated rashly into manless solitudes.
Now without a mate of any kind where am I? that's to say,
Where shall I be to-morrow? where exert my rightful sway
And the purifying strength of my emancipated mind?
Can solitude be lifted up, vacuity refined?
Calling, calling from the shadows in the rear of my
Advance From the Region of Unprogress in the Dark Domain of Chance
Long I heard the Unevolvable beseeching my return
To share the degradation he's reluctant to unlearn.
But I fancy I detected, though I pray it wasn't that

A low reverberation, like an echo in a hat.
So I've held my way regardless, evoluting year by year,
Till I'm what you now behold me or would if you were here
A condensed Emancipation and a Purifier proud
An Independent Entity appropriately loud!
Independent? Yes, in spirit, but (O, woful, woful state!)
Doomed to premature extinction by privation of a mate
To extinction or reversion, for Unexpurgated Man
Still awaits me in the backward if I sicken of the van.
O the horrible dilemma! to be odiously linked
With an Undeveloped Species, or become a Type Extinct!'
As Emancipated Woman wailed her sorrow to the air,
Stalking out of desolation came a being strange and rare
Plato's Man! bipedal, featherless from mandible to rump,
Its wings two quilless flippers and its tail a plumeless stump.
First it scratched and then it clucked, as if in hospitable terms
It invited her to banquet on imaginary worms.
Then it strutted up before her with a lifting of the head,
And in accents of affection and of sympathy it said:
'My estate is some 'at 'umble, but I'm qualified to draw
Near the hymeneal altar and whack up my heart and claw
To Emancipated Anything as walks upon the earth;
And them things is at your service for whatever they are worth.
I'm sure to be congenial, marm, nor e'er deserve a scowl
I'm Emancipated Rooster, I am Expurgated Fowl!'
From the future and its wonders I withdrew my gaze, and then
Wrote this wild unfestive prophecy about the Coming Hen.

An Undress Uniform

The apparel does not proclaim the man
Polonius lied like a partisan,
And Salomon still would a hero seem
If (Heaven dispel the impossible dream!)
He stood in a shroud on the hangman's trap,
His eye burning holes in the black, black cap.
And the crowd below would exclaim amain:
'He's ready to fall for his country again!'

An Unmerry Christmas

Christmas, you tell me, comes but once a year.
One place it never comes, and that is here.
Here, in these pages no good wishes spring,
No well-worn greetings tediously ring
For Christmas greetings are like pots of ore:
The hollower they are they ring the more.
Here shall no holly cast a spiny shade,
Nor mistletoe my solitude invade,

No trinket-laden vegetable come,
No jorum steam with Sheolate of rum.
No shrilling children shall their voices rear.
Hurrah for Christmas without Christmas cheer!
No presents, if you please, I know too well
What Herbert Spencer, if he didn't tell
(I know not if he did) yet might have told
Of present-giving in the days of old,
When Early Man with gifts propitiated
The chiefs whom most he doubted, feared and hated,
Or tendered them in hope to reap some rude
Advantage from the taker's gratitude.
Since thus the Gift its origin derives
(How much of its first character survives
You know as well as I) my stocking's tied,
My pocket buttoned - with my soul inside.
I save my money and I save my pride.
Dinner? Yes; thank you - just a human body
Done to a nutty brown, and a tear toddy
To give me appetite; and as for drink,
About a half a jug of blood, I think,
Will do; for still I love the red, red wine,
Coagulating well, with wrinkles fine
Fretting the satin surface of its flood.
O tope of kings - divine Falernian-blood!
Duse take the shouting fowls upon the limb,
The kneeling cattle and the rising hymn!
Has not a pagan rights to be regarded
His heart assaulted and his ear bombarded
With sentiments and sounds that good old Pan
Even in his demonium would ban?
No, friends, no Christmas here, for I have sworn
To keep my heart hard and my knees unworn.
Enough you have of jester, player, priest:
I as the skeleton attend your feast,
In the mad revelry to make a lull
With shaken finger and with bobbing skull.
However you my services may flout,
Philosophy disdain and reason doubt,
I mean to hold in customary state,

My dismal revelry and celebrate
My yearly rite until the crack o' doom,
Ignore the cheerful season's warmth and bloom
And cultivate an oasis of gloom.

Another Plan
Editor Owen, of San Jose,
Commonly known as 'our friend J.J.'

Weary of scribbling for daily bread,
Weary of writing what nobody read,
Slept one day at his desk and dreamed
That an angel before him stood and beamed
With compassionate eyes upon him there.
Editor Owen is not so fair
In feature, expression, form or limb
But glances like that are familiar to him;
And so, to arrive by the shortest route
At his visitor's will he said, simply: 'Toot.'
'Editor Owen,' the angel said,
'Scribble no more for your daily bread.
Your intellect staggers and falls and bleeds,
Weary of writing what nobody reads.
Eschew now the quill in the coming years
Homilize man through his idle ears.
Go lecture!' 'Just what I intended to do,'
Said Owen. The angel looked pained and flew.
Editor Owen, of San Jose,
Commonly known as 'our friend J.J.'
Scribbling no more to supply his needs,
Weary of writing what nobody reads,
Passes of life each golden year
Speaking what nobody comes to hear.

Another Way

I lay in silence, dead. A woman came
And laid a rose upon my breast, and said,
'May God be merciful.' She spoke my name,
And added, 'It is strange to think him dead.
'He loved me well enough, but 't was his way
To speak it lightly.' Then, beneath her breath:
'Besides' I knew what further she would say,
But then a footfall broke my dream of death.
To-day the words are mine. I lay the rose
Upon her breast, and speak her name, and deem
It strange indeed that she is dead. God knows
I had more pleasure in the other dream.

Arbor Day

Hasten, children, black and white
Celebrate the yearly rite.
Every pupil plant a tree:
It will grow some day to be
Big and strong enough to bear
A School Director hanging there.

Arboriculture

You may say they won't grow, and say they'll decay
Say it again till you're sick of the say,
Get up on your ear, blow your blaring bazoo
And hire a hall to proclaim it; and you
May stand on a stump with a lifted hand
As a pine may stand or a redwood stand,
And stick to your story and cheek it through.
But I point with pride to the far divide
Where the Snake from its groves is seen to glide
To Mariposa's arboreal suit,
And the shaggy shoulders of Shasta Butte,
And the feathered firs of Siskiyou;
And I swear as I sit on my marvelous hair
I roll my marvelous eyes and swear,
And sneer, and ask where would your forests be
To-day if it hadn't been for me!
Then I rise tip-toe, with a brow of brass,
Like a bully boy with an eye of glass;
I look at my gum sprouts, red and blue,
And I say it loud and I say it low:
'They know their man and you bet they'll grow!'

Arma Virumque

'Ours is a Christian Army'; so he said
A regiment of bangomen who led.
'And ours a Christian Navy,' added he
Who sailed a thunder-junk upon the sea.
Better they know than men unwarlike do
What is an army and a navy, too.
Pray God there may be sent them by-and-by
The knowledge what a Christian is, and why.
For somewhat lamely the conception runs
Of a brass-buttoned Jesus firing guns.

Art

For Gladstone's portrait five thousand pounds
Were paid, 't is said, to Sir John Millais.
I cannot help thinking that such fine pay
Transcended reason's uttermost bounds.
For it seems to me uncommonly queer
That a painted British stateman's price
Exceeds the established value thrice
Of a living statesman over here.

Arthur Mcewen

Posterity with all its eyes
Will come and view him where he lies.
Then, turning from the scene away
With a concerted shrug, will say:
'H'm, Scarabaeus Sisyphus
What interest has that to us?
We can't admire at all, at all,
A tumble-bug without its ball.'
And then a sage will rise and say:
'Good friends, you err, turn back, I pray:
This freak that you unwisely shun
Is bug and ball rolled into one.'

Aspiration

Lo! the wild rabbit, happy in the pride
Of qualities to meaner beasts denied,
Surveys the ass with reverence and fear,
Adoring his superior length of ear,
And says: 'No living creature, lean or fat,
But wishes in his heart to be like That!'

At Anchor

The soft asphaltum in the sun;
Betrays a tendency to run;
Whereas the dog that takes his way
Across its course concludes to stay.

At The Close Of The Canvass

'Twas a Venerable Person, whom I met one Sunday morning,
All appareled as a prophet of a melancholy sect;
And in a jeremaid of objurgatory warning
He lifted up his jodel to the following effect:
O ye sanguinary statesmen, intermit your verbal tussles
O ye editors and orators, consent to hear my lay!
And a little while the digital and maxillary muscles
And attend to what a Venerable Person has to say.
Cease your writing, cease your shouting, cease your wild unearthly lying;
Cease to bandy such expressions as are never, never found
In the letter of a lover; cease 'exposing' and 'replying'
Let there be abated fury and a decrement of sound.
For to-morrow will be Monday and the fifth day of November
Only day of opportunity before the final rush.

Carpe diem! go conciliate each person who's a member
Of the other party, do it while you can without a blush.
'Lo! the time is close upon you when the madness of the season
Having howled itself to silence, like a Minnesota 'clone,
Will at last be superseded by the still, small voice of reason,
When the whelpage of your folly you would willingly disown.
'Ah, 'tis mournful to consider what remorses will be thronging,
With a consciousness of having been so ghastly indiscreet,
When by accident untoward two ex-gentlemen belonging
To the opposite political denominations meet!
'Yes, 'tis melancholy, truly, to forecast the fierce, unruly
Supersurging of their blushes, like the flushes upon high
When Aurora Borealis lights her circumpolar palace
And in customary manner sets her banner in the sky.
'Each will think: 'This falsifier knows that I too am a liar.
Curse him for a son of Satan, all unholily compound!
Curse my leader for another! Curse that pelican, my mother!
Would to God that I when little in my victual had been drowned!"
Then that Venerable Person went away without returning
And, the madness of the season having also taken flight,
All the people soon were blushing like the skies to crimson burning
When Aurora Borealis fires her premises by night.

At The Eleventh Hour

As through the blue expanse he skims
On joyous wings, the late
Frank Hutchings overtakes Miss Sims,
Both bound for Heaven's high gate.
In life they loved and (God knows why
A lover so should sue)
He slew her, on the gallows high
Died pious and they flew.
Her pinions were bedraggled, soiled
And torn as by a gale,
While his were bright, all freshly oiled
The feathers of his tail.
Her visage, too, was stained and worn
And menacing and grim;
His sweet and mild, you would have sworn
That she had murdered him.
When they'd arrived before the gate
He said to her: 'My dear,
'Tis hard once more to separate,
But you can't enter here.
'For you, unluckily, were sent
So quickly to the grave
You had no notice to repent,
Nor time your soul to save.'
''Tis true,' said she, 'and I should wail

In Hell even now, but I
Have lingered round the county jail
To see a Christian die.'

At The 'National Encampment'

You 're grayer than one would have thought you:
The climate you have over there
In the East has apparently brought you
Disorders affecting the hair,
Which, pardon me, seems a thought spare.
You'll not take offence at my giving
Expression to notions like these.
You might have been stronger if living
Out here in our sanative breeze.
It's unhealthy here for disease.
No, I'm not as plump as a pullet.
But that's the old wound, you see.
Remember my paunching a bullet?
And how that it didn't agree
With - well, honest hardtack for me.
Just pass me the wine - I've a helly
And horrible kind of drouth!
When a fellow has that in his belly
Which didn't go in at his mouth
He's hotter than all Down South!
Great Scott! what a nasty day that was
When every galoot in our crack
Division who didn't lie flat was
Dissuaded from further attack
By the bullet's felicitous whack.
'Twas there that our major slept under
Some cannon of ours on the crest,
Till they woke him by stilling their thunder,
And he cursed them for breaking his rest,
And died in the midst of his jest.
That night - it was late in November
The dead seemed uncommonly chill
To the touch; and one chap I remember
Who took it exceedingly ill
When I dragged myself over his bill.
Well, comrades, I'm off now, good morning.
Your talk is as pleasant as pie,
But, pardon me, one word of warning:
Speak little of self, say I.
That's my way. God bless you. Good-bye.

Authority

'Authority, authority!' they shout
Whose minds, not large enough to hold a doubt,
Some chance opinion ever entertain,
By dogma billeted upon their brain.
'Ha!' they exclaim with choreatic glee,
'Here's Dabster if you won't give in to me
Dabster, sir, Dabster, to whom all men look
With reverence!' The fellow wrote a book.
It matters not that many another wight
Has thought more deeply, could more wisely write
On t' other side that you yourself possess
Knowledge where Dabster did but faintly guess.
God help you if ambitious to persuade
The fools who take opinion ready-made
And 'recognize authorities.' Be sure
No tittle of their folly they'll abjure
For all that you can say. But write it down,
Publish and die and get a great renown
Faith! how they'll snap it up, misread, misquote,
Swear that they had a hand in all you wrote,
And ride your fame like monkeys on a goat!

Azrael

The moon in the field of the keel-plowed main
Was watching the growing tide:
A luminous peasant was driving his wain,
And he offered my soul a ride.
But I nourished a sorrow uncommonly tall,
And I fixed him fast with mine eye.
'O, peasant,' I sang with a dying fall,
'Go leave me to sing and die.'
The water was weltering round my feet,
As prone on the beach they lay.
I chanted my death-song loud and sweet;
'Kioodle, ioodle, iay!'
Then I heard the swish of erecting ears
Which caught that enchanted strain.
The ocean was swollen with storms of tears
That fell from the shining swain.
'O, poet,' leapt he to the soaken sand,
'That ravishing song would make
The devil a saint.' He held out his hand
And solemnly added: 'Shake.'
We shook. 'I crave a victim, you see,'
He said 'you came hither to die.'
The Angel of Death, 't was he! 't was he!
And the victim he crove was I!
'T was I, Fred Emerson Brooks, the bard;
And he knocked me on the head.

O Lord! I thought it exceedingly hard,
For I didn't want to be dead.
'You'll sing no worser for that,' said he,
And he drove with my soul away,
O, death-song singers, be warned by me,
Kioodle, ioodle, iay!

Bats In Sunshine

Well, Mr. Kemble, you are called, I think,
A great divine, and I'm a great profane.
You as a Congregationalist blink
Some certain truths that I esteem a gain,
And dropp them in the coffers of my brain,
Pleased with the pretty music of their chink.
Perhaps your spiritual wealth is such
A golden truth or two don't count for much.
You say that you've no patience with such stuff
As by Renan is writ, and when you read
(Why do you read?) have hardly strength enough
To hold your hand from flinging the vile screed Into the fire.
That were a wasteful deed
Which you'd repent in sackcloth extra rough;
For books cost money, and I'm told you care
To lay up treasures Here as well as There.
I fear, good, pious soul, that you mistake
Your thrift for toleration. Never mind:
Renan in any case would hardly break
His great, strong, charitable heart to find
The bats and owls of your myopic kind
Pained by the light that his ideas make.
'Tis Truth's best purpose to shine in at holes
Where cower the Kembles, to confound their souls!

Beecher

So, Beecher's dead. His was a great soul, too
Great as a giant organ is, whose reeds
Hold in them all the souls of all the creeds
That man has ever taught and never knew.
When on this mighty instrument He laid
His hand Who fashioned it, our common moan
Was suppliant in its thundering. The tone
Grew more vivacious when the Devil played.
No more those luring harmonies we hear,
And lo! already men forget the sound.
They turn, retracing all the dubious ground
O'er which it led them, pigwise, by the ear.

Bereavement

A Countess (so they tell the tale)
Who dwelt of old in Arno's vale,
Where ladies, even of high degree,
Know more of love than of A.B.C,
Came once with a prodigious bribe
Unto the learned village scribe,
That most discreet and honest man
Who wrote for all the lover clan,
Nor e'er a secret had betrayed
Save when inadequately paid.
'Write me,' she sobbed, 'I pray thee do
A book about the Prince di Giu
A book of poetry in praise
Of all his works and all his ways;
The godlike grace of his address,
His more than woman's tenderness,
His courage stern and lack of guile,
The loves that wantoned in his smile.
So great he was, so rich and kind,
I'll not within a fortnight find
His equal as a lover. O,
My God! I shall be drowned in woe!'
'What! Prince di Giu has died!' exclaimed
The honest man for letters famed,
The while he pocketed her gold;
'Of what'? if I may be so bold.'
Fresh storms of tears the lady shed:
'I stabbed him fifty times,' she said.

Bimetalism

Ben Bulger was a silver man,
Though not a mine had he:
He thought it were a noble plan
To make the coinage free.
'There hain't for years been sech a time,'
Said Ben to his bull pup,
'For biz, the country's broke and I'm
The hardest kind of up.
'The paper says that that's because
The silver coins is sea'ce,
And that the chaps which makes the laws
Puts gold ones in their place.
'They says them nations always be
Most prosperatin' where
The wolume of the currency
Ain't so disgustin' rare.'

His dog, which hadn't breakfasted,
Dissented from his view,
And wished that he could swell, instead,
The volume of cold stew.
'Nobody'd put me up,' said Ben,
'With patriot galoots
Which benefits their feller men
By playin' warious roots;
'But havin' all the tools about,
I'm goin' to commence
A-turnin' silver dollars out
Wuth eighty-seven cents.
'The feller takin' 'em can't whine:
(No more, likewise, can I):
They're better than the genooine,
Which mostly satisfy.
'It's only makin' coinage free,
And mebby might augment
The wolume of the currency
A noomerous per cent.'
I don't quite see his error nor
Malevolence prepense,
But fifteen years they gave him for
That technical offense.

'Black Bart'
Welcome, good friend; as you have served your term,
And found the joy of crime to be a fiction,
I hope you'll hold your present faith, stand firm
And not again be open to conviction.
Your sins, though scarlet once, are now as wool:
You've made atonement for all past offenses,
And conjugated, 'twas an awful pull!
The verb 'to pay' in all its moods and tenses.
You were a dreadful criminal, by Heaven,
I think there never was a man so sinful!
We've all a pinch or two of Satan's leaven,
But you appeared to have an even skinful.
Earth shuddered with aversion at your name;
Rivers fled backward, gravitation scorning;
The sea and sky, from thinking on your shame,
Grew lobster-red at eve and in the morning.
But still red-handed at your horrid trade
You wrought, to reason deaf, and to compassion.
But now with gods and men your peace is made
I beg you to be good and in the fashion.
What's that? you 'ne'er again will rob a stage'?
What! did you do so? Faith, I didn't know it.
Was that what threw poor Themis in a rage?

I thought you were convicted as a poet!
I own it was a comfort to my soul,
And soothed it better than the deepest curses,
To think they'd got one poet in a hole
Where, though he wrote, he could not print, his verses.
I thought that Welcker, Plunkett, Brooks, and all
The ghastly crew who always are begriming
With villain couplets every page and wall,
Might be arrested and 'run in' for rhyming.
And then Parnassus would be left to me,
And Pegasus should bear me up it gaily,
Nor down a steep place run into the sea,
As now he must be tempted to do daily.
Well, grab the lyre-strings, hearties, and begin:
Bawl your harsh souls all out upon the gravel.
I must endure you, for you'll never sin
By robbing coaches, until dead men travel.

Borrowed Brains
Writer folk across the bay
Take the pains to see and say
All their upward palms in air:
'Joaquin Miller's cut his hair!'
Hasten, hasten, writer folk
In the gutters rake and poke,
If by God's exceeding grace
You may hit upon the place
Where the barber threw at length
Samson's literary strength.
Find it, find it if you can;
Happy the successful man!
He has but to put one strand
In his beaver's inner band
And his intellect will soar
As it never did before!
While an inch of it remains
He will noted be for brains,
And at last ('twill so befall)
Fit to cease to write at all.

Business
Two villains of the highest rank
Set out one night to rob a bank.
They found the building, looked it o'er,
Each window noted, tried each door,
Scanned carefully the lidded hole
For minstrels to cascade the coal

In short, examined five-and-twenty
Good paths from poverty to plenty.
But all were sealed, they saw full soon,
Against the minions of the moon.
'Enough,' said one: 'I'm satisfied.'
The other, smiling fair and wide,
Said: 'I'm as highly pleased as you:
No burglar ever can get through.
Fate surely prospers our design
The booty all is yours and mine.'
So, full of hope, the following day
To the exchange they took their way
And bought, with manner free and frank,
Some stock of that devoted bank;
And they became, inside the year,
One President and one Cashier.
Their crime I can no further trace
The means of safety to embrace,
I overdrew and left the place.

By A Defeated Litigant
Liars for witnesses; for lawyers brutes
Who lose their tempers to retrieve their suits;
Cowards for jurors; and for judge a clown
Who ne'er took up the law, yet lays it down;
Justice denied, authority abused,
And the one honest person the accused
Thy courts, my country, all these awful years,
Move fools to laughter and the wise to tears.

By False Pretenses
John S. Hittell, whose sovereign genius wields
The quill his tributary body yields;
The author of an opera that is,
All but the music and libretto's his:
A work renowned, whose formidable name,
Linked with his own, repels the assault of fame
From the high vantage of a dusty shelf,
Secure from all the world except himself;
Who told the tale of 'Culture' in a screed
That all might understand if some would read;
Master of poesy and lord of prose,
Dowered, like a setter, with a double nose;
That one for Erato, for Clio this;
He flushes both, not his fault if we miss;
Judge of the painter's art, who'll straight proclaim
The hue of any color you can name,

And knows a painting with a canvas back
Distinguished from a duck by the duck's quack;
This thinker and philosopher, whose work
Is famous from Commercial street to Turk,
Has got a fortune now, his talent's meed.
A woman left it him who could not read,
And so went down to death's eternal night
Sweetly unconscious that the wretch could write.

Cain
Lord, shed thy light upon his desert path,
And gild his branded brow, that no man spill
His forfeit life to balk thy holy will
That spares him for the ripening of wrath.
Already, lo! the red sign is descried,
To trembling jurors visibly revealed:
The prison doors obediently yield,
The baffled hangman flings the cord aside.
Powell, the brother's blood that marks your trail
Hark, how it cries against you from the ground,
Like the far baying of the tireless hound.
Faith! to your ear it is no nightingale.
What signifies the date upon a stone?
To-morrow you shall die if not to-day.
What matter when the Avenger choose to slay
Or soon or late the Devil gets his own.
Thenceforth through all eternity you'll hold
No one advantage of the later death.
Though you had granted Ralph another breath
Would he to-day less silent lie and cold?
Earth cares not, curst assassin, when you die;
You never will be readier than now.
Wear, in God's name, that mark upon your brow,
And keep the life you purchased with a lie!

California
Why should he not have been allowed
To thread with peaceful feet the crowd
Which filled that Christian street?
The Decalogue he had observed,
From Faith in Jesus had not swerved,
And scorning pious platitudes,
He saw in the Beatitudes
A lamp to guide his feet.
He knew that Jonah downed the whale
And made no bones of it. The tale
That Ananias told

He swore was true. He had no doubt
That Daniel laid the lions out.
In short, he had all holiness,
All meekness and all lowliness,
And was with saints enrolled.
'Tis true, some slight excess of zeal
Sincerely to promote the weal
Of this most Christian state
Had moved him rudely to divide
The queue that was a pagan's pride,
And in addition certify
The Faith by making fur to fly
From pelt as well as pate?
But, Heavenly Father, thou dost know
That in this town these actions go
For nothing worth a name.
Nay, every editorial ass,
To prove they never come to pass
Will damn his soul eternally,
Although in his own journal he
May read the printed shame.
From bloody hands the reins of pow'r
Fall slack; the high decisive hour
Strikes not for liars' ears.
Remove, O Father, the disgrace
That stains our California's face,
And consecrate to human good
The strength of her young womanhood
And all her golden years!

Carmelite

As Death was a-riding out one day,
Across Mount Carmel he took his way,
Where he met a mendicant monk,
Some three or four quarters drunk,
With a holy leer and a pious grin,
Ragged and fat and as saucy as sin,
Who held out his hands and cried:
'Give, give in Charity's name, I pray.
Give in the name of the Church. O give,
Give that her holy sons may live!'
And Death replied,
Smiling long and wide:
'I'll give, holy father, I'll give thee a ride.'
With a rattle and bang
Of his bones, he sprang
From his famous Pale Horse, with his spear;
By the neck and the foot
Seized the fellow, and put

Him astride with his face to the rear.
The Monarch laughed loud with a sound that fell
Like clods on the coffin's sounding shell:
'Ho, ho! A beggar on horseback, they say,
Will ride to the devil!' and thump
Fell the flat of his dart on the rump
Of the charger, which galloped away.
Faster and faster and faster it flew,
Till the rocks and the flocks and the trees that grew
By the road were dim and blended and blue
To the wild, wide eyes
Of the rider in size
Resembling a couple of blackberry pies.
Death laughed again, as a tomb might laugh
At a burial service spoiled,
And the mourners' intentions foiled
By the body erecting
Its head and objecting
To further proceedings in its behalf.
Many a year and many a day
Have passed since these events away.
The monk has long been a dusty corse,
And Death has never recovered his horse.
For the friar got hold of its tail,
And steered it within the pale
Of the monastery gray,
Where the beast was stabled and fed
With barley oil and bread
Till fatter it grew than the fattest friar,
And so in due course was appointed Prior.

Censor Literarum

So, Parson Stebbins, you've released your chin
To say that here, and here, we press folk ail.
'Tis a great thing an editor to skin
And hang his faulty pelt upon a nail
(If over-eared, it has, at least, no tail)
And, for an admonition against sin,
Point out its maculations with a rod,
And act, in short, the gentleman of God.
'Twere needless cruelty to spoil your sport
By comment, critical or merely rude;
But you, too, have, according to report,
Despite your posing as a holy dude,
Imperfect spiritual pulchritude
For so severe a judge. May't please the court,
We shall appeal and take our case at once
Before that higher court, a taller dunce.
Sir, what were you without the press?

What spreads The fame of your existence, once a week,
From the Pacific Mail dock to the Heads,
Warning the people you're about to wreak
Upon the human ear your Sunday freak?
Whereat the most betake them to their bed
Though some prefer to slumber in the pews
And nod assent to your hypnotic views.
Unhappy man! can you not still your tongue
When (like a luckless brat afflict with worms,
By cruel fleas intolerably stung,
Or with a pang in its small lap) it squirms?
Still must it vulgarize your feats of lung?
No preaching better were, the sun beneath,
If you had nothing there behind your teeth.

Charles And Peter
Ere Gabriel's note to silence died
All graves of men were gaping wide.
Then Charles A. Dana, of 'The Sun,'
Rose slowly from the deepest one.
'The dead in Christ rise first, 't is writ,'
Quoth he 'ick, bick, ban, doe, I'm It!'
(His headstone, footstone, counted slow,
Were 'ick' and 'bick,' he 'ban' and 'doe':
Of beating Nick the subtle art
Was part of his immortal part.)
Then straight to Heaven he took his flight,
Arriving at the Gates of Light.
There Warden Peter, in the throes
Of sleep, lay roaring in the nose.
'Get up, you sluggard!' Dana cried
'I've an engagement there inside.'
The Saint arose and scratched his head.
'I recollect your face,' he said.
'(And, pardon me, 't is rather hard),
But' Dana handed him a card.
'Ah, yes, I now remember-bless
My soul, how dull I am I, yes, yes,
'We've nothing better here than bliss.
Walk in. But I must tell you this:
'We've rest and comfort, though, and peace.'
'H'm, puddles,' Dana said, 'for geese.
'Have you in Heaven no Hell?' 'Why, no,'
Said Peter, 'nor, in truth, below.
''T is not included in our scheme
'T is but a preacher's idle dream.'
The great man slowly moved away.
'I'll call,' he said, 'another day.
'On earth I played it, o'er and o'er,

And Heaven without it were a bore.'
'O, stuff! come in. You'll make,' said Pete,
'A hell where'er you set your feet.'

Christian

I dreamed I stood upon a hill, and, lo!
The godly multitudes walked to and fro
Beneath, in Sabbath garments fitly clad,
With pious mien, appropriately sad,
While all the church bells made a solemn din
A fire-alarm to those who lived in sin.
Then saw I gazing thoughtfully below,
With tranquil face, upon that holy show
A tall, spare figure in a robe of white,
Whose eyes diffused a melancholy light.
'God keep you, stranger,' I exclaimed. 'You are
No doubt (your habit shows it) from afar;
And yet I entertain the hope that you,
Like these good people, are a Christian too.'
He raised his eyes and with a look so stern
It made me with a thousand blushes burn
Replied his manner with disdain was spiced:
'What! I a Christian? No, indeed! I'm Christ.'

Codex Honoris

Jacob Jacobs, of Oakland, he swore:
'Dat Solomon Martin, I'll haf his gore!'
Solomon Martin, of Oakland, he said:
'Of Shacob Shacobs der bleed I vill shed!'
So they met, with seconds and surgeon at call,
And fought with pistol and powder and all
Was done in good faith, as before I said,
They fought with pistol and powder and shed
Tears, O my friends, for each other they marred
Fighting with pistol and powder and lard!
For the lead had been stolen away, every trace,
And Christian hog-product supplied its place.
Then the shade of Moses indignant arose:
'Quvicker dan lighdnings go vosh yer glose!'
Jacob Jacobs, of Oakland, they say,
Applied for a pension the following day.
Solomon Martin, of Oakland, I hear,
Will call himself Colonel for many a year.

Consolation

Little's the good to sit and grieve
Because the serpent tempted Eve.
Better to wipe your eyes and take
A club and go out and kill a snake.
What do you gain by cursing Nick
For playing her such a scurvy trick?
Better go out and some villain find
Who serves the devil, and beat him blind.
But if you prefer, as I suspect,
To philosophize, why, then, reflect:
If the cunning rascal upon the limb
Hadn't tempted her she'd have tempted him.

Constancy

Dull were the days and sober,
The mountains were brown and bare,
For the season was sad October
And a dirge was in the air.
The mated starlings flew over
To the isles of the southern sea.
She wept for her warrior lover
Wept and exclaimed: 'Ah, me!
'Long years have I mourned my darling
In his battle-bed at rest;
And it's O, to be a starling,
With a mate to share my nest!'
The angels pitied her sorrow,
Restoring her warrior's life;
And he came to her arms on the morrow
To claim her and take her to wife.
An aged lover, a portly,
Bald lover, a trifle too stiff,
With manners that would have been courtly,
And would have been graceful, if
If the angels had only restored him
Without the additional years
That had passed since the enemy bored him
To death with their long, sharp spears.
As it was, he bored her, and she rambled
Away with her father's young groom,
And the old lover smiled as he ambled
Contentedly back to the tomb.

Contemplation

I muse upon the distant town
In many a dreamy mood.
Above my head the sunbeams crown

The graveyard's giant rood.
The lupin blooms among the tombs.
The quail recalls her brood.
Ah, good it is to sit and trace
The shadow of the cross;
It moves so still from place to place
O'er marble, bronze and moss;
With graves to mark upon its arc
Our time's eternal loss.
And sweet it is to watch the bee
That reve's in the rose,
And sense the fragrance floating free
On every breeze that blows
O'er many a mound, where, safe and sound,
Mine enemies repose.

Contentment
Sleep fell upon my senses and I dreamed
Long years had circled since my life had fled.
The world was different, and all things seemed
Remote and strange, like noises to the dead.
And one great Voice there was; and something said:
'Posterity is speaking rightly deemed
Infallible:' and so I gave attention,
Hoping Posterity my name would mention.
'Illustrious Spirit,' said the Voice, 'appear!
While we confirm eternally thy fame,
Before our dread tribunal answer, here,
Why do no statues celebrate thy name,
No monuments thy services proclaim?
Why did not thy contemporaries rear
To thee some schoolhouse or memorial college?
It looks almighty queer, you must acknowledge.'
Up spake I hotly: 'That is where you err!'
But some one thundered in my ear: 'You shan't
Be interrupting these proceedings, sir;
The question was addressed to General Grant.'
Some other things were spoken which I can't
Distinctly now recall, but I infer,
By certain flushings of my cheeks and forehead,
Posterity's environment is torrid.
Then heard I (this was in a dream, remark)
Another Voice, clear, comfortable, strong,
As Grant's great shade, replying from the dark,
Said in a tone that rang the earth along,
And thrilled the senses of the Judges' throng:
'I'd rather you would question why, in park
And street, my monuments were not erected
Than why they were.' Then, waking, I reflected.

Convalescent

What! 'Out of danger?' Can the slighted Dame
Or canting Pharisee no more defame?
Will Treachery caress my hand no more,
Nor Hatred lie alurk about my door?
Ingratitude, with benefits dismissed,
Not understanding what 'tis all about,
Will Envy henceforth not retaliate
For virtues it were vain to emulate?
Will Ignorance my knowledge fail to scout,
Not understanding what 'tis all about,
Yet feeling in its light so mean and small
That all his little soul is turned to gall?
What! 'Out of danger?' Jealousy disarmed?
Greed from exaction magically charmed?
Ambition stayed from trampling whom it meets.
Like horses fugitive in crowded streets?
The Bigot, with his candle, book and bell,
Tongue-tied, unlunged and paralyzed as well?
The Critic righteously to justice haled,
His own ear to the post securely nailed
What most he dreads unable to inflict,
And powerless to hawk the faults he's picked?
The Liar choked upon his choicest lie,
And impotent alike to vilify
Or flatter for the gold of thrifty men
Who hate his person but employ his pen
Who love and loathe, respectively, the dirt
Belonging to his character and shirt?
What! 'Out of danger?' Nature's minions all,
Like hounds returning to the huntsman's call,
Obedient to the unwelcome note
That stays them from the quarry's bursting throat?
Famine and Pestilence and Earthquake dire,
Torrent and Tempest, Lightning, Frost and Fire,
The soulless Tiger and the mindless Snake,
The noxious Insect from the stagnant lake,
These from their immemorial prey restrained,
Their fury baffled and their power chained?
I'm safe? Is that what the physician said?
What! 'Out of danger?' Then, by Heaven, I'm dead!

Cooperation

No more the swindler singly seeks his prey;
To hunt in couples Is the modern way
A rascal, from the public to purloin,

An honest man to hide away the coin.

Corrected News

'T was a maiden lady (the newspapers say)
Pious and prim and a bit gone gray.
She slept like an angel, holy and white,
Till ten o' the clock in the shank o' the night
(When men and other wild animals prey)
And then she cried in the viewless gloom:
'There's a man in the room, a man in the room!'
And this maiden lady (they make it appear)
Leapt out of the window, five fathom sheer!
Alas, that lying is such a sin
When newspaper men need bread and gin
And none can be had for less than a lie!
For the maiden lady a bit gone gray
Saw the man in the room from across the way,
And leapt, not out of the window but in
Ten fathom sheer, as I hope to die!

Couplets

I am for Cutting. I'm a blade
Designed for use at dress parade.
My gleaming length, when I display
Peace rules the land with gentle sway;
But when the war-dogs bare their teeth
Go seek me in the modest sheath.
I am for Cutting. Not for me
The task of setting nations free.
Let soulless blades take human life,
My softer metal shuns the strife.
The annual review is mine,
When gorgeous shopmen sweat and shine,
And Biddy, tip-toe on the pave,
Adores the cobble-trotting brave.
I am for Cutting. 'Tis not mine
To hew amain the hostile line;
Not mine all pitiless to spread
The plain with tumuli of dead.
My grander duty lies afar
From haunts of the insane hussar,
Where charging horse and struggling foot
Are grimed alike with cannon-soot.
When Loveliness and Valor meet
Beneath the trees to dance, and eat,
And sing, and much beside, behold
My golden glories all unfold!

There formidably are displayed
The useful horrors of my blade
In time of feast and dance and ballad,
I am for cutting chicken salad.

Creation
God dreamed, the suns sprang flaming into place,
And sailing worlds with many a venturous race!
He woke. His smile alone illumined space.

De Young - A Prophecy
Running for Senator with clumsy pace,
He stooped so low, to win at least a place,
That Fortune, tempted by a mark so droll,
Sprang in an kicked him to the winning pole.

Decalogue
Thou shalt no God but me adore:
'Twere too expensive to have more.
No images nor idols make
For Roger Ingersoll to break.
Take not God's name in vain: select
A time when it will have effect.
Work not on Sabbath days at all,
But go to see the teams play ball.
Honor thy parents. That creates
For life insurance lower rates.
Kill not, abet not those who kill;
Thou shalt not pay thy butcher's bill.
Kiss not thy neighbor's wife, unless
Thine own thy neighbor doth caress.
Don't steal; thou'lt never thus compete
Successfully in business. Cheat.
Bear not false witness, that is low
But 'hear 'tis rumored so and so.'
Covet thou naught that thou hast got
By hook or crook, or somehow, got.

Democracy
Let slaves and subjects with unvaried psalms
Before their sovereign execute salaams;
The freeman scorns one idol to adore
Tom, Dick and Harry and himself are four.

Dennis Kearney

Your influence, my friend, has gathered head
To east and west its tides encroaching spread.
There'll be, on all God's foot-stool, when they meet,
No clean spot left for God to set His feet.

Detected

In Congress once great Mowther shone,
Debating weighty matters;
Now into an asylum thrown,
He vacuously chatters.
If in that legislative hall
His wisdom still he 'd vented,
It never had been known at all
That Mowther was demented.

Diagnosis

Cried Allen Forman: 'Doctor, pray
Compose my spirits' strife:
O what may be my chances, say,
Of living all my life?
'For lately I have dreamed of high
And hempen dissolution!
O doctor, doctor, how can I
Amend my constitution?'
The learned leech replied: 'You're young
And beautiful and strong
Permit me to inspect your tongue:
H'm, ah, ahem! 'tis long.'

'Died Of A Rose'

A reporter he was, and he wrote, wrote he:
'The grave was covered as thick as could be
With floral tributes' which reading,
The editor man he said, he did so:
'For 'floral tributes' he's got for to go,
For I hold the same misleading.'
Then he called him in and he pointed sweet
To a blooming garden across the street,
Inquiring: 'What's them a-growing?'
The reporter chap said: 'Why, where's your eyes?
Them's floral tributes!' 'Arise, arise,'

The editor said, 'and be going.'

Dies Irae
Dies irae! dies ilia!
Solvet saeclum in favilla
Teste David cum Sibylla.
Quantus tremor est futurus,
Quando Judex est venturus.
Cuncta stricte discussurus.
Tuba mirum spargens sonum
Per sepulchra regionem,
Coget omnes ante thronum.
Mors stupebit, et Natura,
Quum resurget creatura
Judicanti responsura.
Liber scriptus proferetur,
In quo totum continetur,
Unde mundus judicetur.
Judex ergo quum sedebit,
Quicquid latet apparebit,
Nil inultum remanebit.
Quid sum miser tunc dicturus,
Quem patronem rogaturus,
Quum vix justus sit securus?
Rex tremendae majestatis,
Qui salvandos salvas gratis;
Salva me, Fons pietatis
Recordare, Jesu pie
Quod sum causa tuae viae;
Ne me perdas illa die.
Quarens me sedisti lassus
Redimisti crucem passus,
Tantus labor non sit cassus.
Juste Judex ultionis,
Donum fac remissionis
Ante diem rationis.
Ingemisco tanquam reus,
Culpa rubet vultus meus;
Supplicanti parce, Deus.
Qui Mariam absolvisti
Et latronem exaudisti,
Mihi quoque spem dedisti.

Preces meae non sunt dignae,
Sed tu bonus fac benigne
Ne perenni cremer igne.
Inter oves locum praesta.
Et ab haedis me sequestra,
Statuens in parte dextra.

Confutatis maledictis,
Flammis acribus addictis,
Voca me cum benedictis.
Oro supplex et acclinis,
Cor contritum quasi cinis;
Gere curam mei finis.
Lacrymosa dies illa
Qua resurgent et favilla,
Judicandus homo reus
Huic ergo parce, Deus!

Disappointment

The Senate woke; the Chairman's snore
Was stilled, its echoes balking;
The startled members dreamed no more,
For Steele, who long had held the floor,
Had suddenly ceased talking.
As, like Elijah, in his pride,
He to his seat was passing,
'Go up thou baldhead!' Reddy cried.
Then six fierce bears ensued and tried
To sunder him for 'sassing.'
Two seized his legs, and one his head,
The fourth his trunk, to munch on;
The fifth preferred an arm instead;
The last, with rueful visage, said:
'Pray what have I for luncheon?'
Then to that disappointed bear
Said Steele, serene and chipper,
'My friend, you shall not lack your share:
Look in the Treasury, and there
You'll find his other flipper.'

Discretion
SHE:
I'm told that men have sometimes got
Too confidential, and
Have said to one another what
They - well, you understand.
I hope I don't offend you, sweet,
But are you sure that you're discreet?
HE:
'Tis true, sometimes my friends in wine
Their conquests do recall,
But none can truly say that mine
Are known to him at all.
I never, never talk you o'er

In truth, I never get the floor.

Down Among The Dead Men
Within my dark and narrow bed
I rested well, new-laid:
I heard above my fleshless head
The grinding of a spade.
A gruffer note ensued and grew
To harsh and harsher strains:
The poet Welcker then I knew
Was 'snatching' my remains.
'O Welcker, let your hand be stayed
And leave me here in peace.
Of your revenge you should have made
An end with my decease.'
'Hush, Mouldyshanks, and hear my moan:
I once, as you're aware,
Was eminent in letters known
And honored everywhere.
'My splendor made all Berkeley bright
And Sacramento blind.
Men swore no writer e'er could write
Like me - if I'd a mind.
'With honors all insatiate,
With curst ambition smit,
Too far, alas! I tempted fate
I published what I'd writ!
'Good Heaven! with what a hunger wild
Oblivion swallows fame!
Men who have known me from a child
Forget my very name!
'Even creditors with searching looks
My face cannot recall;
My heaviest one - he prints my books
Oblivious most of all.
'O I should feel a sweet content
If one poor dun his claim
Would bring to me for settlement,
And bully me by name.
'My dog is at my gate forlorn;
It howls through all the night,
And when I greet it in the morn
It answers with a bite!'
'O Poet, what in Satan's name
To me's all this ado?

Will snatching me restore the fame
That printing snatched from you?'
'Peace, dread Remains; I'm not about

To do a deed of sin.
I come not here to hale you out
I'm trying to get in.'

Egotist

Megaceph, chosen to serve the State
In the halls of legislative debate,
One day with his credentials came
To the capitol's door and announced his name.
The doorkeeper looked, with a comical twist
Of the face, at the eminent egotist,
And said: 'Go away, for we settle here
All manner of questions, knotty and queer,
And we cannot have, when the speaker demands
To know how every member stands,
A man who to all things under the sky
Assents by eternally voting 'I.''

Election Day

Despots effete upon tottering thrones
Unsteadily poised upon dead men's bones,
Walk up! walk up! the circus is free,
And this wonderful spectacle you shall see:
Millions of voters who mostly are fools
Demagogues' dupes and candidates' tools,
Armies of uniformed mountebanks,
And braying disciples of brainless cranks.
Many a week they've bellowed like beeves,
Bitterly blackguarding, lying like thieves,
Libeling freely the quick and the dead
And painting the New Jerusalem red.
Tyrants monarchical - emperors, kings,
Princes and nobles and all such things
Noblemen, gentlemen, step this way:
There's nothing, the Devil excepted, to pay,
And the freaks and curios here to be seen
Are very uncommonly grand and serene.
No more with vivacity they debate,
Nor cheerfully crack the illogical pate;
No longer, the dull understanding to aid,
The stomach accepts the instructive blade,
Nor the stubborn heart learns what is what
From a revelation of rabbit-shot;
And vilification's flames - behold!
Burn with a bickering faint and cold.
Magnificent spectacle! every tongue
Suddenly civil that yesterday rung

(Like a clapper beating a brazen bell)
Each fair reputation's eternal knell;
Hands no longer delivering blows,
And noses, for counting, arrayed in rows.
Walk up, gentlemen - nothing to pay
The Devil goes back to Hell to-day.

Elegy

The cur foretells the knell of parting day;
The loafing herd winds slowly o'er the lea;
The wise man homewards plods; I only stay
To fiddle-faddle in a minor key.

Elixer Vitæ

Of life's elixir I had writ, when sleep
(Pray Heaven it spared him who the writing read!)
Settled upon my senses with so deep
A stupefaction that men thought me dead.
The centuries stole by with noiseless tread,
Like spectres in the twilight of my dream;
I saw mankind in dim procession sweep
Through life, oblivion at each extreme.
Meanwhile my beard, like Barbarossa's growing,
Loaded my lap and o'er my knees was flowing.
The generations came with dance and song,
And each observed me curiously there.
Some asked: 'Who was he?' Others in the throng
Replied: 'A wicked monk who slept at prayer.'
Some said I was a saint, and some a bear
These all were women. So the young and gay,
Visibly wrinkling as they fared along,
Doddered at last on failing limbs away;
Though some, their footing in my beard entangled,
Fell into its abysses and were strangled.
At last a generation came that walked
More slowly forward to the common tomb,
Then altogether stopped. The women talked
Excitedly; the men, with eyes a-gloom
Looked darkly on them with a look of doom;
And one cried out: 'We are immortal now
How need we these?' And a dread figure stalked,
Silent, with gleaming axe and shrouded brow,
And all men cried: 'Decapitate the women,
Or soon there'll be no room to stand or swim in!'
So (in my dream) each lovely head was chopped
From Its fair shoulders, and but men alone
Were left in all the world. Birth being stopped,

Enough of room remained in every zone,
And Peace ascended Woman's vacant throne.
Thus, life's elixir being found (the quacks
Their bread and butter in it gladly sopped)
'Twas made worth having by the headsman's axe.
Seeing which, I gave myself a hearty shaking,
And crumbled all to powder in the waking.

Ambrose Bierce – A Short Biography

Ambrose Gwinnett Bierce had a diverse literary, military and journalistic career, during which his sardonic view of human nature ensured he was both frequently critical and frequently criticised. As a writer, his work included short stories, fables, editorials and his journalism, which was often controversial owing to his vehemence and acerbic style.

He was born on June 24th 1842 to Marcus Aurelius Bierce (1799-1876) and Laura Sherwood Bierce at Horse Cave Creek in Meigs Country, Ohio. Though his parents were poor they were literarily inclined and they introduced Bierce to this passion at an early age, instilling in him a deep appreciation of books, the written word and the elegance of language.

Bierce grew up in Koscuisko Country, Indiana, attending school at the county seat in Warsaw. He was the tenth of thirteen children, all of whom Marcus Aurelius gave names beginning with 'A', an indication of his love of poetry and alliteration. In order of birth they were Abigail, Amelia, Ann, Addison, Aurelius, Augustus, Almeda, Andrew, Albert, Ambrose, Arthur, Adelia and Aurelia. Poverty and religion were defining features of his childhood, and he would later describe his parents as "unwashed savages" and fanatically religious, showing him little affection but quick to punish him "with anything they could lay their hand on". He soon came to resent religion, and an introduction to literature is about the only lasting effect Marcus Aurelius had on Bierce.

Instead, Bierce began to respect his Uncle Lucius, whose "political and military distinction won the admiration of his nephew"; as an important figure within the American military and a graduate of Ohio University, he seemed far more worthy of admiration than his father. The family moved Westward when he was nine "in search of better land, and a more promising future", settling on 80 acres of farmland in Walnut Creek, Indiana.

Then, at the age of fifteen, Bierce left home to become a printer's devil, mixing ink and fetching type at The Northern Indian, a small Ohio newspaper run by a man named Reuben Williams. The duration of his time here is uncertain, though it is known that he quit the apprenticeship; apparently after being falsely accused of a theft. He returned to the family farm and spent time sending work to editors in the hopes of being published, though he was met with frequent rejection.

On the recommendation of his Uncle Lucius he was sent to the Kentucky Military Institute where, after a year's education, he was commissioned as an Officer in the Union Army. At the outset of the American Civil War in 1861, Bierce enlisted in the Union Army's 9th Indiana Infantry Regiment. His first major participation was during the Operations in Western Virginia campaign of 1861, and he was present at the 'first battle' at Philippi.

At the Battle of Rich Mountain on July 11th 1861 he executed the daring rescue of a gravely wounded comrade under heavy enemy fire, an act of bravery which received attention in the newspaper.

Following this triumph he was commissioned First Lieutenant, serving as a topographical engineer on the staff of General William Babcock Hazen, undertaking the important work of making maps of likely battlefields.

In April 1862 Bierce fought at the Battle of Shiloh, an experience which, though terrifying, became the source of several of his short stories in later years, along with the memoir What I Saw of Shiloh. Two more years of valuable service followed until June 1864 when, while fighting at the Battle of Kennesaw Mountain, he sustained a serious head wound which required him to spend the summer on furlough, an unpaid yet honourable period of leave, in order to recover. He returned to active duty in September of that year, only to be discharged in January 1865 towards the close of the war.

However midway through 1866 he rejoined General Hazen on his expedition to inspect military outposts across the Great Plains, proceeding by horseback and wagon from Omaha, Nebraska, to San Francisco, California, at the end of the year.

While still in San Francisco, Bierce was presented with the rank of brevet major before tendering his resignation from the Army, choosing to remain in San Francisco and becoming involved with publishing and editing. On Christmas Day of 1871 Bierce married Mary Ellen, also known as Molly, with whom he had his first child, Day, the following year.

Later in 1872 he moved to England where he lived and wrote between the years 1872 and 1875, contributing work to Fun magazine. In 1874 his second son, Leigh, was born, and while in England he saw his first book, The Fiend's Delight, published by John Camden Hotton under the pseudonym 'Dod Grile'. It appeared in London in 1873, and was a collection of his articles. On the back of this success he was published twice more, first Nuggets and Dust Panned Out in California in 1873, and the next year Cobwebs from and Empty Skull, both collections of stories, fables, maxims, sketches, poetry, epigrams, quips and witticisms.

After this success and his continued regular contribution to Fun, he returned to San Francisco where he took up a more permanent residence and focused on his editorial career, working for a number of local papers including The San Francisco News Letter, The Argonaut, the Overland Monthly, The Californian and The Wasp. His crime writing was some of the finest of the medium and was reproduced in the Library of America anthology True Crime. His novella 'The Dance of Death', co-written with Thomas A. Harcourth for which he used the pseudonym William Herman was published in 1877, and then from 1879 to 1880 he travelled to the Dakota Territory, visiting Rockerville and Deadwood and experimenting with a managerial role at a New York mining company.

With the failure of that company he returned to San Francisco to continue his journalism, where in 1887 he began a column at the San Francisco Examiner named 'Prattle', which saw him become one of William Randolph Hearst's first regular columnists and editors at the paper. He eventually became one of the more influential and prominent of the journalists and writers of the West Coast. His association with Hearst Newspapers would continue until 1906.

Bierce's marriage was to fall apart when in 1888 he discovered compromising letters to his wife from a secret admirer. This led to their separation. The following year, 1889 his first son Day committed suicide following depression brought on by a romantic rejection.

In 1891, inspired by his time in the Union Army, Bierce wrote and published the collection of 26 short stories, Tales of Soldiers and Civilians which included his famous 'An Occurrence at Owl Creek Bridge'. Maintaining in the preface to the first edition that the book had been "denied existence by the chief publishing houses in the country", the eventual publication is accredited to his friend Mr

E.L.G. Steele, a San Franciscan merchant against whose name the 1891 copyright is listed. The heavy irony of his depictions of battlefield heroism and valour perhaps reflects his own response to the differences between his act of human bravery, rescuing a comrade, and the 'brave sacrifices' of troop leaders whose stubborn and rash decisions often led to the deaths of many whose lives could have been spared by more prudent warmongering. A particular example of this is found in the actions of Lieutenant Brayle, of the story 'Incident at Resaca', in whose orders for a hundred men to charge gloriously into certain death Bierce presents valourous sacrifice, ideally rendered, but it is a portrayal which he then juxtaposes against the gruesomely realistic descriptions of their wounds and deaths. Moreover, alongside these informed accounts of battlefield brutality he acknowledges the frequent injuries sustained by women and children which were oft overlooked by official accounts and propaganda.

Three more publications followed, a book of poetry in 1892 entitled Black Beetles in Amber, followed by a novella, again co-written but this time with Adolphe De Castro named The Monk and the Hangman's Daughter, also published in 1892 and Can Such Things Be?, a collection of short stories which reached print in 1893. By this time the Union Pacific and Central Pacific railroad companies were receiving huge loans from the United States Government towards their endeavours to build the First Transcontinental Railroad, and Collis P. Huntingdon sought to introduce a bill which quietly excused the companies from repaying the money, essentially converting the loan into a handout of $130 million dollars. The plot's essence was secrecy, for its perpetrators hoped to get the bill through Congress without any public notice and subsequent hearing, so in 1896 Hearst dispatched Bierce to Washington, D.C to scupper their plans. Confronted by Huntingdon on the steps of the Capitol and angrily invited to name his price, Bierce answered "my price is $130 million dollars. If, when you are ready to pay, I happen to be out of town, you may hand it over to my friend, the Treasurer of the United States". This answer became famous and was recorded in newspapers nationwide, and his coverage of and diatribes on the issue encouraged such public outrage that the bill was challenged and defeated. Following this huge success, Bierce returned to California in November.

He now began his first foray into a career as a fabulist, publishing Fantastic Fables in 1899 and anticipating the rise of ironic grotesquerie which was seen in the 20th century. The following year, owing to his penchant for stirring up the public through his biting satire and social criticism, he induced a hostile reaction to a poem he had written in 1900 about the assassination of Governor Goebel and following the assassination of President William McKinley which had been deliberately misconstrued by Hearst's opponents, turning it into something of a cause célèbre. The poem was meant to express the national sense of fear and dismay at Goebel's death, but the lines

> The bullet that pierced Goebel's breast
> Can not be found in all the West;
> Good reason, it is speeding here
> To stretch McKinley on his bier

(written innoculously in 1900) seemed to foreshadow the subsequent shooting on McKinley in 1901. This saw Hearst accused of having called for McKinley's assassination by his rivals and then by Elihu Root, then Secretary of State, though despite the national uproar which ended Hearst's ambitions for presidency, Bierce was never revealed as the author of the poem; nor, indeed, did Hearst ever fire him from the paper.

In 1901, his second son Leigh died of pneumonia relating to his alcoholism.

His enduring career at the paper was accompanied by several more publications, the next of which was Shapes of Clay in 1903, a book of poetry and the first publication of one of his most famous works, The Devil's Dictionary, which began life as an occasional newspaper item of satirical definitions of English words and then, in 1906, was published as a collection in book form under the name The Cynic's Word Book. In 1909 The Cynic's Word Book was reprinted under its current name, which Bierce himself preferred, as the entirety of the seventh volume of his Collected Works which brought together the majority of his short stories and poems. The same year he wrote Write it Right, a non-fiction work of literary criticism and commentary, which appeared alongside The Shadow on the Dial, and other essays. However, despite this professional success he finally divorced his wife in 1904, and she died the following year.

At the age of 71, in 1913 Bierce departed from Washington, D.C., for a tour of the battlefields upon which he had fought during the civil war. He had passed through Louisiana and Texas by December and was crossing into by way of El Paso into Mexico which was itself in the throes of revolution. He joined Pancho Villa's army as an observer in Ciudad Juárez during which time he witnessed the battle of Tierra Blanca. It is known that he accompanied Villa's army as far as the city of Chihuahua where he wrote his last known communication in the form of a letter to Blanche Partington, one of his close friends, dated 26th December 1913. He closed the letter with the words "as to me, I leave here tomorrow for an unknown destination" and then vanished without trace in what would become one of the most famous unexplained disappearances in American history. Various suggestions have been posited, including that belonging to the oral tradition of Sierra Mojada, Coahuila, which holds that Bierce was executed by firing squad in the town cemetery there. All that is known is that, by this time, he was suffering considerably from the asthma which had dogged him throughout his life and was compounded by his war injuries.

In 1920, three of his stories A Horseman in the Sky, A Watcher by the Dead and The Man and the Snake were published posthumously, and further poetry was published in 1980 under the title A Vision of Doom: Poems by Ambrose Pierce. As a writer, he often found himself splitting opinion and continues to do so in death, his writing variously described as cheap and vulgar, and conversely the best writing on war and that of a flawless American genius. Regardless of how differently his critics speak of him, his legacy is one of concise, acerbic and cruelly satirical social commentary, an authorial style of economy, fruitful observation and as a judicious wordsmith.

www.ingramcontent.com/pod-product-compliance
Lightning Source LLC
Chambersburg PA
CBHW071722040426
42446CB00011B/2172